YORK NO

General Editors: Professo ___ (*University of Stirling*) & *Professor Su* ___ *ushrui* (*American University of Beirut*)

Voltaire

CANDIDE

Notes by Colin Niven

MA (CAMBRIDGE)
Head of Modern Languages, Sherborne School

LONGMAN
YORK PRESS

Extracts from the English translation of *Candide* by John Butt
are reprinted by kind permission of Penguin Books Ltd

YORK PRESS
Immeuble Esseily, Place Riad Solh, Beirut.

LONGMAN GROUP LIMITED
London
Associated companies, branches and representatives
throughout the world

First published 1980
ISBN 0 582 78235 X
Printed in Hong Kong by
Sing Cheong Printing Co Ltd

Contents

Part 1

Introduction

Voltaire's life and times

On 30 May 1878 Victor Hugo paid tribute to Voltaire's memory in these words: 'A hundred years ago a man died. He died immortal . . . He went cursed and blessed; cursed by the past, blessed· by the future . . . He was more than a man, he was an age.'[1] Another century has gone by, and we still share Hugo's admiration and gratitude. 'Ecrasez l'infâme' —crush the infamous—was the battle-cry implicit in all that Voltaire wrote. He was in his lifetime, and remains in ours, the conscience of mankind. With a ferocious grin he ridiculed injustice wherever he saw it. No state or church or individual, however powerful, could frighten him. Rather, he frightened them. As Lord Macaulay said 'Of all the intellectual weapons that have ever been wielded by man, the most terrible was the mockery of Voltaire. Bigots and tyrants who had never been moved by the wailings and cursings of millions, turned pale at his name.'[2]

In his sixty-fifth year Voltaire crystallised his philosophy of life in the short story that has become his most popular work—*Candide*. His lessons are as relevant today as they were in 1759. We laugh as loudly as the eighteenth-century reader and recognise the same absolute truths. As Voltaire said himself: 'I think the best way to fall on the infamous is to seem to have no wish to attack it; . . . to let the reader draw his own conclusions'. From *Candide* we learn the need to be realistic and not to live in a world of fantasy, for only when we face a problem squarely can we hope to solve it. From a host of adventures, some tragic, some hilarious, Voltaire's hero comes to appreciate the value of hard work. We must not just talk, we must act to improve our lives and those of our fellow men. Yet if by some misfortune the manuscript of *Candide* had been destroyed, we would still have read these lessons in the life of Voltaire himself. His honesty, his industry, his courage, his wit, above all, his sense of justice, are as much an inspiration as his masterpiece itself.

The name Voltaire was in fact his own invention, for he was baptised François-Marie Arouet, and adopted his pen-name while he was

[1] Quoted by Victor Thaddeus in his appendix to *Voltaire—genius of mockery*, Brentano's, New York, 1928.
[2] *The Complete Works of Lord Macaulay*, Longman, London, 1928, Vol. IX, p.597.

imprisoned in the Bastille (the formidable prison in the centre of Paris; its fall on 14 July 1789 heralded the French Revolution). He was nominally the son of François Arouet, an official in the tax department in Paris, though he may actually have been the son of the writer Rochebrune (c.1670–1732), a minor poet of the Auvergne, and a frequent visitor at the home of Voltaire's presumed father. He was born on 21 November 1694 and at the age of nine went to the collège Louis-le-grand, a Jesuit School. Here he studied the Greek and Latin classics, wrote his first poems, acted in school plays and became familiar with the Bible.

His Jesuit teachers gave him a general Christian education, but unintentionally contributed to his later deism. By the time he wrote *Candide*, Voltaire had rejected the Catholic view; admittedly he died a Christian, but only to ensure himself a decent burial—unlike the actress in *Candide*. He acknowledged the existence of a Deity who created the world; but Voltaire's God was a remote one who no more loved individual people than the master of the ship worries about the mice on board. Like his King of Eldorado, Voltaire was grateful for the gift of life and wanted to use it for the good of his fellow man. As he says in *L'Epître à Uranie*, 'God judges us by our virtues and not by our sacrifices.' His religion was one of action, not of faith.

All through Voltaire's early life Louis XIV was King of France. In 1751 Voltaire published *Le Siècle de Louis XIV* and paid tribute to his greatness; but in 1715, after a reign of seventy-two years, the King at last died. His successor, Louis XV, was only five years old and a Regency was necessary. Louis XIV had named the Duke of Maine, his natural son, as Regent but the King's nephew, Philip of Orléans, contested the will and was proclaimed. Voltaire intrigued against the new Regent and was exiled to the pleasant château of Sully-sur-Loire. Soon he returned, but a spy, Captain Beauregard, accused him of writing a satirical attack on the Regent, and he was sent to the Bastille for nearly a year.

In prison he began his epic poem, the *Henriade*, in which he condemned the hypocrisy and ambition of the Church, a theme that runs through *Candide*. The poem enjoyed much success, and in 1718 his tragedy *Oedipe* was a triumph and ran, uniquely, for forty-five performances. The play, in which the gods make the unwitting Oedipus commit incest with his mother, was an implied attack on the absolute authority of the Church and the Monarchy of France. Voltaire had sown the seeds of the French Revolution.

Now in his thirties, Voltaire was rich and famous; but not famous enough. A nobleman, Rohan-Chabot, insulted Voltaire's middle-class background, and Voltaire in return mocked the decline of Rohan's family. Rohan's servants subsequently beat him in the street, and when

Voltaire threatened a duel Rohan used his aristocratic influence to have him thrown into the Bastille again. On his release in May 1726 Voltaire left for England, disgusted by this typical abuse of privilege in France.

Thanks to Walpole, the English Ambassador to France,[1] Voltaire met many of the most famous men in England, among them Bolingbroke, Swift, Pope and Gay.[2] He learnt English with extraordinary facility and quickly became one of the first Frenchmen to appreciate the genius of Shakespeare.[3] He admired the precision and profundity of Isaac Newton's[4] laws of physics, and later published a summary of the scientist's ideas, itself a model of clarity. Above all he was impressed by the much greater degree of religious and political freedom—two crucial matters to which he returns again and again in *Candide*—that the English enjoyed in comparison with the French. His *Philosophical Letters* paid homage to England, but inevitably they seemed what they really were, a criticism of France. When, for example, he wrote: 'No doubt the establishment of liberty in England has been costly; it is in seas of blood that the idol of despotic power has been drowned; but the English do not think that they have paid too high a price for their laws' —inevitably the French Court felt threatened, and refused permission to publish the book in France.

In England, too, he started his *Histoire de Charles XII* (1731), a history of the Swedish King, which was unusual in its efforts to be fair and objective. In the preface Voltaire observed that 'disbelief . . . is the basis of all wisdom'. It is a lesson that Candide eventually learns.

Back in France, the ever-practical Voltaire made a fortune from a lottery by the simple method of buying all the tickets! He now wrote *Zaïre* (1732), an Oriental tragedy in which religion proves helpless in the face of passionate love. Again, this is a theme that is echoed often in *Candide*.

As he approached his fortieth birthday, Voltaire himself fell deeply in love with Emilie, marquise du Châtelet. She had remained on good terms with her husband, the Governor of Semur, even after she had taken a number of lovers. She was uncommonly well read and was a

---

[1] Horatio Walpole, later 1st Baron Walpole of Wolverton (1678-1757).
[2] Henry St John, 1st Viscount Bolingbroke (1678-1751), Secretary of State for War under Queen Anne, to whom Voltaire dedicated *Brutus* (1730); Jonathan Swift (1667-1745), Dean of St Patrick's Cathedral, Ireland, and author of *Gulliver's Travels* (1726), which helped to inspire Voltaire's *Micromégas* (1752); Alexander Pope (1688-1744), major English poet and author of *An Essay on Man Addressed to a Friend* (1733) the optimism of which is satirised in *Candide*; John Gay (1685-1732), author of *The Beggar's Opera* (1728), which satirises the vices of London society.
[3] William Shakespeare (1564-1616), now universally recognised as England's greatest poet, was considered uncouth and primitive in Voltaire's time, for he ignored the rigidly formal rules of classical drama, to which French playwrights adhered.
[4] Sir Isaac Newton (1642-1727), author of *Principia* (1687), formulated the law of gravitation and invented the infinitesimal calculus.

gifted mathematician and philosopher. A lady of striking appearance, she lived happily at Cirey with Voltaire until he fell in love with his niece. She sought consolation with Saint Lambert[1], but died in 1749 having given birth to his child.

Voltaire was deeply affected. However, his niece Marie-Louise Denis had captivated him. For the rest of his life Voltaire loved her passionately, forgiving her meanness and her infidelities. From his first love affair in 1713 with Olympe du Noyer, time and again Voltaire knew the exhilaration and suffering that love can cause. Small wonder that Candide lives only to see Cunégonde again. Yet, at the wedding of his friends Richelieu[2] and Mlle de Guise[3], Voltaire had warned the couple that 'it is better to be friends for life than lovers for a day or two'. Again Candide reflects Voltaire's personal experience, for after the first shock of Cunégonde's ugliness, he finds they can live a friendly, useful life together, she as a pastry cook and he as a gardener.

In the happy days with Mme du Châtelet, Voltaire was appointed historiographer to the King, and achieved the high literary honour of a seat in the French Academy. Bishop Mirepoix[4] had vetoed him once, but cunningly Voltaire sought the blessing of Pope Benedict XII, to whom he dedicated his play *Mahomet*, and Mirepoix was suitably impressed. The tragedy, which Voltaire reckoned his best, was a scathing attack on the imperialism that so often lay beneath robes of piety. Candide encounters this very problem in Paraguay among the Jesuit priests.

In France, meanwhile, the clergy, led by Mirepoix, furiously resented Voltaire's suggestion that the Church should pay taxes to lighten the burden of the peasants. Unpopular with the authorities again, and grieved by the death of Mme du Châtelet, Voltaire at last accepted the longstanding invitation of Frederick II of Prussia[5] to join him in Berlin.

Frederick the Great, a musician who also wrote French poetry, deeply admired Voltaire and expressed a desire to become a philosopher-king, rejecting the bloodthirsty methods of other rulers such as his own father. However, when the young Maria Theresa mounted the throne of Austria, he soon saw an opportunity to extend the boundaries of Prussia. Forgetting all his early promises, he confessed in a letter to Voltaire, as he invaded Silesia, 'Glory is a great folly, but a folly too

[1] Jean François, marquis de Saint Lambert (1716–1803) and a minor poet, whose romantic, philosophical work praised the rural life.
[2] Louis François Armand du Plessis, duc de Richelieu (1696–1788) was the great-nephew of Louis XIII's minister, Cardinal Richelieu (1585–1642); a 'maréchal de France', he fought at Fontenoy.
[3] Elisabeth Sophie de Lorraine, duchesse de Guise, married Richelieu in 1734.
[4] Boyer, Bishop of Mirepoix and Tutor to Louis XV's heir, the Dauphin.
[5] Frederick the Great (1712–86): through his military and political skill he increased the power of his Kingdom of Prussia, thereby sowing the seeds of the future German Empire.

difficult to banish once we dote upon it!' Thus he plunged Europe into a devastating war, which on and off for twenty years would reach even America and India. In Voltaire's youth, Louis XIV's army had endured several terrible defeats, and later, despite a memorable victory at Fontenoy in 1745, Louis XV's army had also suffered severely from the attacks of the Austrians, Hanoverians and English. Voltaire tried in vain to persuade Frederick to come to the help of the French. Later this War of the Austrian Succession flared up again from 1756 to 1763, when France and Austria fought against England and Prussia in the Seven Years War. Thus all his life Voltaire witnessed the cruel, stupid slaughter occasioned by war. It is not surprising that so much of *Candide* derides those kings whose vanity causes tragedy in the lives of the innocent.

The uneasy friendship between Voltaire and Frederick was further damaged by a quarrel as to the merits of Maupertuis[1], the Director of the Berlin Academy. A risky business deal that involved Voltaire in a lawsuit did not help, and in 1753 he and the King coldly parted company. Frederick, quite illegally, had Voltaire arrested in Frankfurt, demanding the return of his manuscripts. He escaped into Alsace, and soon after settled in his house, 'Les Délices', in Geneva.

At first, like Candide, he learnt the pleasure of cultivating his garden. He declined an invitation to visit Maria Theresa, saying, 'I shall not go to Vienna. I am too comfortable in my retreat at Les Délices. Lucky the man who lives in his own house with his nieces, his books, his garden, his vines, his horses, his eagle, his fox and his rabbits that rub their noses with their paws . . . I would rather grumble at my gardeners than pay my respects to Kings.'[2]

Yet he had his worries. The authorities, narrow-minded followers of the extreme Protestant Calvin[3], forbade Genevans to visit the theatre that Voltaire built. The philosopher Rousseau[4] began a quarrel that grew steadily more bitter, for he advocated a return to the simple, natural life, whilst Voltaire rejected this idea. He felt, as Eldorado reminds us, that man's powers of reason and his scientific discoveries can improve the world, and that Rousseau's ideas would take us back

---

[1] Pierre Louis Moreau de Maupertuis (1698–1759) was a distinguished scientist who visited Lapland to measure the degree of meridian to verify Newton's description of the shape of the earth. The expedition is parodied in *Micromégas* and Maupertuis is also satirised in Voltaire's *Diatribe du Docteur Akakia* (1752).

[2] Quoted by Theodore Besterman, *Voltaire*, Longman, London, 1968.

[3] Jean Calvin (1509–64), author of *Institutes of the Christian Religion* (1536), a manual of Protestant dogmatic theology; he was a major figure of the Reformation.

[4] Jean Jacques Rousseau (1712–78), author of *Emile ou de l'Education* (1762), *Du Contrat Social* (1762), and *Confessions* (1782) in which he describes art and science as corrupting instruments that serve the rich. He was an inspiration to leaders of the romantic literary movement in France and to the political leaders of the Revolution.

to the level of animals. Thus, with amusing but biting sarcasm, Voltaire parodies Rousseau's theories in *Candide*, and the ladies in the land of the Oreillons fall in love with monkeys. Moreover, Voltaire was continually harassed by untrustworthy printers and booksellers, whilst the authorities regularly burned his works in public.

His personal worries faded into insignificance, however, beside an event that profoundly disturbed Voltaire and led directly to the creation of *Candide*. On 1 November 1755—ironically the Christian Feast of All Saints—an earthquake shattered the capital of Portugal: The lives of thousands of ordinary, unsuspecting people were destroyed or ruined. To Voltaire it was irrefutable proof that no loving God watched over us, and that life was a lottery. The only minimal consolation was that the Inquisitors, whose cruel superstition he ridicules in *Candide*, were also killed with their victims. After the man-made horrors of war this natural disaster rendered absurd, even obscene, in Voltaire's mind the idea that English and German thinkers had expressed: that all was well in God's world. His *Poem on the Lisbon Disaster* and his novel *Candide* destroyed such woolly optimism. In its place he offered hard work and honesty, for these allow man a little real hope of a better world.

In 1756 the same objectivity characterised his *Essai sur l'histoire générale et sur les moeurs et l'esprit des nations*, a voluminous survey of the history of civilisation. As ever, the enlightened law-maker is preferred to the cruel tyrant, anticipating the ideal state of Eldorado. A number of witty short stories and the influential *Dictionnaire Philosophique* (1764) poured scorn on the fantastic aspects of religion, stripping the legend from the historic reality.

At an age when most men retire, Voltaire began a new life. Thin as a skeleton, but his eyes as brilliant and his grin as fierce as ever, Voltaire moved with his niece to Ferney, an impoverished corner of France very close to Geneva. By the time of his death, Voltaire had so carefully administered his estates that a flourishing town gratefully changed its name to Ferney-Voltaire. Industry flourished as watches and stockings were exported all over the world. Roads were built, and a happy, prosperous community blessed the name of the man who practised what he had preached at the end of *Candide*. Frederick the Great again sought his friendship, Catherine II of Russia humbly asked for his advice, and the great men of the world called so frequently at Ferney that Voltaire called himself 'the inn-keeper of Europe'!

As Ferney prospered, France fell into economic chaos under the leadership of Choiseul[1]. By 1774, when the misnamed 'well-beloved'

[1] Etienne François, comte de Stainville, duc de Choiseul (1719–85); as Minister for Foreign Affairs, he dominated Louis XV's government. He restored something of France's fortunes after the Seven Years War, but failed to initiate the reforms that alone could have averted the Revolution.

Louis XV died, she had lost both Canada and India to England, and the Ancien Régime awaited its destruction in the Revolution fifteen years away. For twenty courageous months Turgot[1], the new Minister of Finance, followed the life-long policies of Voltaire, trying to ease the taxation on the peasants and to cut down the privileges of the nobles and clergy; but the inexperienced Louis XVI submitted to the pressure of the wealthy, and threw away his life-line in 1776 when, to Voltaire's sorrow, he dismissed Turgot.

As the Monarchy slumbered, injustice was rife, and many families had cause to thank Voltaire. In 1761 at Toulouse, for instance, Jean Calas[2] was tortured to death after his son was found hanged. It was suicide, but the magistrate claimed that the Protestant father had murdered his son to prevent him from becoming a Catholic. Voltaire's tireless efforts eventually vindicated the family's reputation. In 1765 he persuaded the monarchs of Prussia, Russia, Poland and Denmark to contribute money to his defence of the Sirvens, another Protestant family from near Toulouse, who were accused of killing their daughter, when in fact she had fallen down a well. Six years of determined fighting eventually proved their innocence. Such injustice showed up the religious intolerance of the French legal system.

More horrific still was the judicial murder so often practised for the most trivial offences. In 1766 for example, the young chevalier de la Barre failed to show sufficient respect at a religious procession and to Voltaire's disgust was tortured to death before an appreciative audience, much as Cunégonde describes the Auto da Fé. Candide, in his turn, witnesses with revulsion the execution of Admiral Byng[3] at Portsmouth before another satisfied crowd. Byng had failed to fight La Galissonnière in 1756 off Minorca and, to 'encourage' other English admirals to be more bold, was duly shot. Voltaire, with the help of Richelieu, had tried in vain to save Byng, whom he had briefly met in England. Twenty years later France was guilty of a similar crime. The Comte de Lally-Tollendal[4] was decapitated for surrendering after a heroic struggle against the English in India. Voltaire protested against such savagery, and successfully cleared the Count's name. He could now, he said, die a happy man. The modernisation of the French legal system clearly owes much to Voltaire.

At eighty-three he returned to Paris. It was a fairy-tale ending. His play *Irène* was a triumph in every sense, for at the Comédie-Française

[1] Anne-Robert-Jacques Turgot (1727–81), Comptroller General under Louis XVI, managed to abolish many unjust taxes and privileges, but was ultimately destroyed by the self-interest of the wealthy.
[2] Jean Calas (1698–1762), a cloth merchant.
[3] John Byng (1704–57).
[4] Thomas Arthur, comte de Lally-Tollendal (1702–66) was commander-in-chief of the French army defeated in 1761 at Pondicherry.

a laurel crown was placed on his head. He became Director of the Academy and initiated a new dictionary. He received hundreds of distinguished visitors, including Benjamin Franklin[1], who had just negotiated an alliance between France and the United States in the War of American Independence. On 30 March 1778 Voltaire drove across Paris in a blue coach studded with golden stars through a throng deliriously cheering their hero. Two months later he died. His body was smuggled out of Paris to be given the decent burial he desired. When the Bastille fell, his remains were placed amidst the ruins of that symbol of dictatorship, and then borne in triumph to the Panthéon. With the downfall of Napoleon, the Bourbon royalists and priests returned, and they threw away his bones. It was a worthless gesture of spite, for as Frederick the Great had rightly predicted, his fame was immortal.

The philosophical background

The rapid advance of scientific discovery at the turn of the eighteenth century encouraged many people to assume that mankind was progressing constantly to a better future. The English poet Alexander Pope even claimed in his *Essay on Man* that 'whatever is, is right'; thus anything that seemed evil or painful was in fact another good part of God's plan, which we were simply too ignorant as yet to understand. Voltaire disliked this negative attitude, for if all is well, why bother to improve things? Why dig our garden at all?

The German philosopher Leibniz[2] expressed a view similar to Pope's. Admittedly he recognised that evil was really evil. However, since God had given men the right to choose to be good or bad, then God himself had deliberately made an imperfect creature. Now Leibniz felt that even God was subject to the laws of reason, and so could only create the best of all *possible* worlds—and since man had the capacity to do evil, then even the best of worlds had to contain evil. Voltaire looked with horror at the Lisbon earthquake, a natural disaster for which mankind could not possibly be held responsible, and rejected this optimistic theory in disgust. Professor Christian Wolff[3] of Germany systematised Leibniz's theories in a massive work full of philosophical jargon, which Voltaire ridiculed by creating Pangloss. It seemed to Voltaire particularly absurd that Germans should be preaching optimism, when their country was being mutilated by war.

[1] Benjamin Franklin (1706–90) framed the Constitution of the USA and was also the inventor of the stove, bifocals and the lightning conductor.
[2] Gottfried Wilhelm Leibniz (1646–1716) was a writer on many branches of learning who helped to found the German Academy of Science in Berlin.
[3] Christian, Freiher von Wolff (1679–1754), adviser to Czar Peter the Great at the St Petersburg Academy of Science and later Chancellor of Halle University.

Voltaire found their attitude simply dishonest. How could anyone claim that all was for the best when, as *Candide* amply illustrates, the world is full of earthquakes, tempests, warlike kings, barbaric religions, slavery, prostitution, venereal disease, suffering of every kind, or just plain boredom? Unlike Pangloss, Martin is at least a realist, but his bleak pessimism is ultimately too passive for Voltaire. Martin is a Manichean, a follower of the Persian Manes, who believed that the world was contested by the forces of Good and Evil; to him man is as inevitably evil as a sparrow-hawk is bound to kill sparrows; it is simply in his nature.

Voltaire is more positive. When the dervish slams the door in the face of Pangloss, we are reminded that, however interesting it may be to philosophise, there is work to be done. Furthermore, we should not pray to God to save us, for as the Ingénu, another of Voltaire's innocent heroes, reminds us, we are tiny cogs in God's vast machine; he acts by general laws, not personal ones, and is not concerned with men as individuals. The solution lies then with Man himself.

Voltaire allows us a modicum of hope. In his *Poème sur le Désastre de Lisbonne* he writes:

Un jour tout sera bien, voilà notre espérance,
Tout est bien aujourd'hui, voilà l'illusion.

(One day all will be good, that is our hope,
All is good today, that is the illusion.)

Even this he later modified with a question mark. However, unlike Martin (the principal representation of pessimism in *Candide*), Voltaire still suggests that things may improve, if only men are realistic and industrious and, of course, lucky.

The literary background

Candide superficially follows the traditional pattern of the 'picaresque' novel, which takes the hero and his friends through a breathless succession of adventures, without worrying too much about the psychology of the characters. Voltaire, however, exaggerates this already unsophisticated technique and makes it ludicrous. Events tragic or comic rush by like scenes in a Walt Disney cartoon. The dead spring up again. Every sigh and gesture is larger than life. Coincidences abound. It is very funny of course, but even as we laugh we pause to think. The cheerful tone contrasts so violently with the terrible agony it describes that we are forced to look beneath the surface of things at their true significance. This is exactly what Candide learns to do himself by the end of the book. Thus Voltaire's ironic treatment of the eighteenth-century novel emphasises the moral lessons of his book.

It would be wrong, though, to end on a solemn note. The tone of the 'conte', reaching back beyond Boccaccio[1] and Chaucer[2], was light-hearted. Many names in *Candide* are mildly improper, and the story is full of the sexual yearnings, infidelities and frustrations of the characters. Yet Voltaire is never crude. Everything is suggested rather than stated, and from the first page to the last, in the very best literary traditions, it is great fun.

A note on the text

According to his secretary Jean-Louis Wagnière, Voltaire completed *Candide* in July 1758, during a three-week stay at Schwetzingen where he was a guest of the Elector of the Palatinate, Karl Theodor. No doubt the Lisbon earthquake of 1755 had first prompted the idea. In this minor German court his host and hostess resembled the Baron of Thunder-ten-tronckh and his wife, whilst the seventeen-year-old Prince of Mecklenburg probably provided a model for Candide. By December Voltaire had corrected the text, adding Chapter 19 on the Surinam slave.

In January 1759 Gabriel Cramer published the first edition in Geneva. Both there and in Paris the Church protested, and the book was banned. Even so it sold six thousand copies in Paris within weeks. Voltaire, partly for fun, partly for self-preservation, denied he had written it, attributing it to the fictitious German Dr Ralph. Later he improved his picture of Paris in Chapter 22, and in 1761 produced the definitive text. Only in 1768 did he admit he was the author. By his death some fifty editions had already appeared.

Candide has enjoyed unfailing popularity ever since. It appears most recently in an edition edited by René Pomeau, Nizet, Paris, 1959; in J.H. Brumfitt's edition, Oxford University Press, London, 1968; in Roland Barthe's and José Lupin's *Voltaire — Romans et Contes*, Gallimard, Paris, 1972; in H. Bénac's *Voltaire — Romans et Contes*, Garnier, Paris, 1960; and in English in John Butt's translation, Penguin Books, Harmondsworth, 1947.

To help both those who read *Candide* in the original French and those who read it in an English translation, quotations are given in each language. Many good French editions are available, and the chapters are conveniently short, so after the French quotations only the chapter is given. English quotations have a page reference from the excellent Penguin translation by John Butt.

[1] Giovanni Boccaccio (1313-75), Italian author of *The Decameron* (1348-53), a bawdy, cheerful, essentially humanist collection of tales that raised the vernacular to a literary level.
[2] Geoffrey Chaucer (c. 1342-1400), English courtier and poet, wrote *The Canterbury Tales* (c. 1390) which philosophise with earthy humour about spiritual and physical love.

Part 2

Summaries
of CANDIDE

A general summary

Candide is as innocent as his name suggests. Thanks to his tutor, Pangloss, he thinks that the castle where he lives is perfect and that in fact everything is ideal in an ideal world. Gradually his adventures, many of which are very funny, open his eyes to reality, and in the end he rejects Pangloss's woolly optimism. He admits that there is much that is wrong with the world, but he finds in hard work a real consolation amid the sorrows of life.

Almost everywhere in the old world of Europe and the new one of America he comes upon misery.

His colourful acquaintances offer him a choice of philosophies that range from the extreme optimism of Pangloss to the bleak pessimism of Martin, or from the loving selflessness of Jacques to the brutal selfishness of the drunken sailor.

Only Eldorado seems a truly peaceful, religious and happy community. Yet he arrives there by only good luck, and decides very quickly to leave this earthly paradise.

This is because of Cunégonde. From the first time he kisses her in the castle till the moment he meets her again in Constantinople, Candide adores the lovely girl, and the memory of her fills him with hope and gives him a purpose in life.

When he finds her, though, she has become very ugly. Yet after a period of deadly boredom, Candide, Cunégonde, Martin, Pangloss, Paquette, Giroflée and that remarkably down-to-earth old woman, the Pope's daughter—but not the snobbish Baron, for he is a Jesuit!—all live reasonably contented lives, since they have learnt the lesson that 'we must cultivate our garden'.

Detailed summaries

Chapter 1

How Candide was brought up in a beautiful castle and how he was thrown out of it.

In Baron Thunder-ten-tronckh's 'castle', which, unlike most other

Westphalian buildings actually has a door and windows, lives a young man called Candide. He is as charmingly innocent as he looks.

The Baron's family are very snobbish. His sister, who is generally considered Candide's mother, refused to marry Candide's father because his amazingly noble background was still not good enough. The Baron's 'court' in fact consists of the local villagers. The Baroness owes her dignity to her colossal figure. Their son is thoroughly 'worthy' of his father; and their daughter is a delectable seventeen-year-old, Cunégonde.

She is tutored by Pangloss, an 'expert' in just about everything; he teaches that everything is caused by something, and that all is for the best in the best of all possible worlds. For instance, noses were made so that we can wear glasses, feet so that we can wear shoes, stones so we can make castles, and the Baron's is 'therefore' the best possible castle.

Candide swallows it all, for his attention is distracted by Cunégonde. And when one day she finds Pangloss doing some 'experimental physics'—or rather, physical experiments—with a chamber-maid, she quickly decides she too would like to experience these 'causes and effects'. Behind a screen she drops her handkerchief for Candide to pick up; one thing leads to another, their knees tremble, their hands wander. . . . The Baron catches them, Candide is kicked out, and all is consternation in the best of all possible castles!

NOTES AND GLOSSARY:

Westphalia: a flat, poor part of Germany that Voltaire had crossed on his way to Prussia. The pompous Baron, with his grand titles for ordinary things, reflects the snobbery of the petty German aristocracy. Sixty-four quarterings on the family shield is the most possible, yet Candide's father has seventy-one and still is not noble enough

hunting: a nobleman hunted stags, boar and foxes with his pack of hounds

Candide, Cunégonde, Pangloss, Thunder-ten-tronckh: these names are symbolic. 'Candide' suggests innocence. 'Cunégonde', though a noble name, also hints at sex. 'Pangloss' means 'all tongue' in Greek, for he can explain away any problem. 'Thunder-ten-tronckh' suggests 'violent wind in the trunk, or body', an amusingly vulgar reminder of the harsh sounds of the German language

tutor: a private tutor educated the children of a rich family at home

metaphysico-theologo-cosmolo-nigology: Pangloss's subjects satirise the heavy titles of Wolff's works. Metaphysics are the study of existence and knowledge; theology is the study of God; cosmology is the study of the universe; and nigology is an invented word that suggests that all Pangloss's teaching is a fraud

He proved incontestably . . .: Like Wolff, Pangloss teaches the principle of 'sufficient reason'. He says that every 'effect' has a 'cause'. In other words, everything happens for a reason. That reason is God's plan for mankind. Therefore, even if an individual suffers, it is necessary if God is to achieve his overall purpose. Therefore, even suffering is good. Voltaire, who hated to see others suffer, finds this nonsense, and thus satirises these theories by showing how Pangloss's arguments turn the world upside down

Candide listened . . . with implicit belief: Pangloss uses words like 'because' and 'therefore', which sound impressive but in fact are illogical. Notice that Candide believes Pangloss, 'for' he is attracted to Cunégonde: Voltaire parodies Pangloss's style and shows that Candide is not really listening!

experimental physics: Voltaire again parodies Wolff's style: Pangloss is making love

---

Chapter 2

What happened to Candide among the Bulgars.

Frozen, famished and lamenting his 'Paradise Lost', Candide comes to Waldberghoff-trarbk-dikdorff. Two men in blue—in fact recruiting officers for the King of the Bulgars—'very kindly' invite him to dinner. They all agree that men exist to help one another. Candide gladly drinks the King's health, and suddenly finds himself in chains. He is drilled at fantastic speed and beaten thirty times; next day, twenty; the third 'only' ten. He does not relish the role of a 'hero'; he reckons that human beings, like any animal, have the right to walk away freely, but the army does not agree. He protests in vain about man's free will; they offer him a choice between thirty-six thrashings from the 2000 soldiers and the firing squad. He chooses the former, but after being nearly skinned alive he asks if they would mind shooting him instead. By chance, the King appears, recognises Candide's innocent nature, and pardons him. A doctor, using ancient methods, cures him in time for the war against the Abars.

NOTES AND GLOSSARY:

paradise: Candide is thrown out of his 'earthly paradise', much as Adam is banished from the Garden of Eden in the Bible. Later he realises that Eldorado is the real paradise. At the end of the story he comes to a garden which, if not Eden, is at least much more satisfying than the 'castle' in Westphalia

Waldberghoff-trarbk-dikdorff: the name means 'the dense village of Trarbk by the farm near the mountain wood', another parody of the German language

Bulgars: while Voltaire was writing *Candide*, the Prussians were fighting the French in the Seven Years War. Like the Bulgars they wore blue uniforms, so the King represents Frederick. The Abars, then, are the French. In fact, the Abars were an Asian tribe who conquered the Bulgars in the sixth century. Voltaire suggests that modern kings are really as primitive as those of ancient days

men in blue: Frederick sought soldiers of at least five feet five inches in height, that is 1m 80. All over Europe kings 'pressed-ganged' innocent citizens into military service against their will. In the army the drill was exhausting. Deserters had to 'run the gauntlet' like Candide; the victim was thrashed by a line of men holding the ramrods with which they usually loaded their guns

Free Will: Candide at first believes in free will. Voltaire, on the other hand, felt that generally speaking our actions are so limited by our situation, that they are largely predetermined. Candide soon learns that the King's will counts for more than his own

cured: Candide is cured in a miraculously short time. In reality he would surely have died. This emphasises Voltaire's irony, for Dioscorides lived in the first century AD and French medicine clearly needs reform

chance: Candide's naïvety enables the soldiers to deceive him. Yet the same innocence persuades the King—who anyway appears in time only by chance—to reprieve him. Voltaire suggests that life is a gamble

Chapter 3

What happened to Candide after he escaped from the Bulgars.

The two armies present a glorious, ordered spectacle. The music and gunfire create a harmony hell itself has never known. The guns and bayonets are the 'sufficient reason'—or cause—of the deaths of some thirty thousand rogues who infect this best of all possible worlds. Candide trembles in terror 'like a philosopher' during this heroic butchery. Eventually both camps sing a hymn of victory!

Candide visits a ruined village on either side. Everywhere he sees the same horrible massacre of young and old, male and female, as a result of the 'heroic' soldiers' lust and blood-thirstiness.

Still inspired by the thought of Cunégonde, he seeks for Christian charity in Holland. He is immediately warned against begging. A preacher asks if he thinks the Pope is the Devil. Candide has no ideas on the subject: he just wants food. The preacher's wife empties her bedpan on him for his 'opinions'.

Mercifully, Jacques (James), the Anabaptist, gives him shelter and offers him a job with a 'Dutch manufacturer of Persian materials'.

Candide is reassured in his faith in Pangloss's optimism, but next day he meets a horribly mutilated, diseased beggar.

NOTES AND GLOSSARY:

display: warfare was very formal at this time. The rival armies in their bright uniforms faced each other openly and kept their formations even under fire

Te Deums: the 'Te Deum' is the Christian hymn of thanksgiving. Clearly the armies cannot both have won

international law: Voltaire felt that the 'droit public' or international law could not prevent atrocities, just as they still occur in modern warfare despite the Geneva Convention

the Pope: Holland was Protestant and based its Christianity directly on Christ's teaching. Thus the Pope, who to the Catholics is God's representative on earth, seems to the Dutch preacher to be the 'Antichrist'

Persian silks: the Dutch merchants are deceiving the public. They sell what seem to be the best silks—those from Persia—when in fact they make them themselves

Anabaptist: the Anabaptists were Christians who baptised only adults, for they thought children too young to understand. Voltaire admired the way they practised what they preached. Jacques is as helpful to Candide as the Good Samaritan in Christ's parable

Chapter 4

How Candide met his old Philosophy teacher, Dr Pangloss.

Candide compassionately gives the beggar the money he had received from Jacques. Amazed, he realises it is Pangloss. He learns that Cunégonde has been raped 'as much as possible', and that the family and castle have been destroyed. However, the Abars took their revenge and did the same to a Bulgar village.

Pangloss explains the 'sufficient reason' for his condition: it was 'love', or more precisely, venereal disease, which he had contracted from Paquette, the chamber-maid. He traces the disease to its source, one of the sailors with Columbus; now, whilst discovering chocolate and cochineal in America, Columbus picked up the infection, so we owe these luxuries to syphilis, so it is a good and necessary thing. Pangloss is confident it will soon spread everywhere.

Jacques pays for his cure and they set sail for Lisbon on business. The one-eyed philosopher argues that personal misfortune contributes to the general good, so the more unhappiness there is, the happier people are. Jacques disagrees; he feels that men are born pure but grow corrupt—after all, we are not born with guns.

While they are talking, they run into a violent storm.

NOTES AND GLOSSARY:

hellish torments: Pangloss suffers from syphilis, a disease caused by lack of hygiene, usually as a result of indiscriminate sexual intercourse. If affects the blood, horribly marks the face, often leads to madness and can destroy the health of the victim's descendants. Thus it governs the actions of many kings, priests, politicians and soldiers who, in their madness, cause much wider misery than even the venereal disease itself. Voltaire is not just commenting on Pangloss's morals. He urges better medical care. Already in his *English Letters* he had advised France to follow England's example and inoculate people against smallpox, a similarly terrible disease

Columbus: Christopher Columbus's crew is supposed to have brought syphilis back from America after discovering the continent. The 'family tree' of venereal disease is a comment on the widespread immorality of the times, and is a comic reminder of the Baron's snobbish fixation about heredity

Chapter 5

Storm, shipwreck, earthquake and what became of Dr Pangloss, Candide and the Anabaptist Jacques.

The boat disintegrates. The passengers scream, pray or are paralysed with fear. Jacques tries to steer, but is attacked by a furious sailor, who nearly falls in. Jacques, in saving him, loses his own life, which does not bother the sailor at all. Candide is shocked, but Pangloss 'proves' that Lisbon's waters were made for Jacques to drown in. The ship sinks and only the sailor, Pangloss and Candide survive.

In the city an earthquake destroys most buildings and a tidal wave crushes the ships in the port. Thirty thousand people are killed. Pangloss seeks an explanation for the phenomenon; Candide thinks it is the end of the world; and the sailor, unconcerned about Pangloss's 'universal reason', loots the city.

Pangloss ignores the desperate cries of the wounded Candide for oil and wine, and compares the cause and effect of this earthquake with the recent one in Lima. When Candide recovers, he explains to the survivors how good it all is, as the volcano is in Lisbon, which means it cannot be anywhere else, so all is well.

An officer of the Inquisition concludes from this that he does not believe in original sin and the Fall of Adam, or in free will. Pangloss says free-will and the Fall are predetermined in an ideal universe ... but before he can finish he is arrested.

NOTES AND GLOSSARY:

good and evil: the innocent passengers and the good Jacques die; yet the evil sailor is saved. Voltaire emphasises that there is no divine justice to watch over men; life is a matter of chance

Pangloss: Pangloss argues *a priori*. He presupposes his idea (that all is for the best) to be true. The shipwreck immediately disproves his theory. As ever, Pangloss talks when he should be acting

trample on the crucifix: after expelling the Europeans, the Japanese traded only with those who were prepared to walk on the crucifix, the symbol of Christianity. The sailor did this, yet goes unpunished

Inquisition: the Inquisition was the terrifying court of justice of the Roman Catholic Church in Portugal, Spain and Italy. It punished hundreds of heretics and Jews with death

Free Will:　　　　Pangloss believes in 'original sin'; he thinks that because Adam disobeyed God, man is doomed to eternal punishment, unless Christ saves him. As he also thinks everything is good, then man's fall must be good too. No wonder the Inquisition is suspicious! Pangloss also believes in man's free will; his right to choose between good and evil. Yet he also believes in 'absolute necessity'; the idea that everything is predestined

Chapter 6

How an auto-da-fé was held to prevent earthquakes and how Candide was thrashed.

The University of Coimbra decides on an auto-da-fé to prevent another earthquake. They arrest a Biscay man for marrying his godchild's godmother; two Portuguese Jews for not eating fat; and Candide and Pangloss. After a week in the cells—'lodgings of extreme freshness'— they are dressed in cassocks and mitres, decorated with flames and devils, and are punished to the beautiful sounds of chanting. Candide is thrashed, Pangloss hanged ('though it is not the custom') and the others burned. That day there is another earthquake.

Candide thinks of his miseries and wonders what the other worlds are like if this is really the best. An old woman bids him follow her.

NOTES AND GLOSSARY:

auto-da-fé:　　　Coimbra was the centre of the Inquisition in Portugal. Heretics were usually burned to death in an auto-da-fé, the Spanish for 'act of faith'. Voltaire ridicules the superstitious ceremony. Thus the flames on Pangloss's 'san-benito', his yellow robes, point upwards, for his opinions differed from those of the Inquisition; Candide's flames point downwards, for he merely listened to such 'heresy'. The 'faux bourdon' music, written in counter-point for several voices, is as beautiful as the ceremony is cruel

Basque:　　　　this man, from the Basque country that overlaps France and Spain, has broken the law of the church in marrying the godmother of the child, whose godfather he was. As there is no blood relationship, Voltaire considers this law absurd

Jews:　　　　　by eating no fat, these Portuguese prove they are Jews, the constant victims of the Inquisition

Chapter 7

How an old woman cared for Candide, and how he rediscovered the one he loved.

She gives him ointment, feeds and clothes him, and gives him a bed. Later she leads the grateful Candide to a lovely house, and leaves him in a golden room. She returns with a trembling woman, who is veiled and bedecked with jewels. What a surprise! It is Cunégonde! They faint, are revived, sigh, weep and express their amazement. She agrees that her family were massacred, but though she herself was indeed raped and disembowelled, 'you don't always die of these two accidents'. Candide, in a faltering voice, tells his story and then, unable to tear his eyes away from Cunégonde, listens to her tale.

NOTES AND GLOSSARY:

Our Lady of Atocha, etc.: Our Lady of Atocha was portrayed by a statue in Madrid, which reputedly wept on the saint's day. St Antony of Padua was the patron saint of Portugal, and St James of Compostella (and of Santiago) the patron saint of Spain. The Pope's daughter, as the old woman turns out to be, of course knows her saints! However, Voltaire never took them seriously, and these three do not seem to protect Candide with much enthusiasm!

Chapter 8

Cunégonde's tale.

Cunégonde describes the invasion of her family's castle. Unaware that he was 'only behaving normally', she resisted a huge Bulgar as he raped her. He then stabbed her, and she promises she will show Candide the wound.

The soldier failed to stand up when a Bulgar Captain came in. So the officer killed him and took Cunégonde prisoner; she still recalls the whiteness of his skin. He sold her to a Jewish banker, Don Issachar, but she claims to have resisted him: 'An honourable person can be raped once, but it reinforces her virtue!' Later, threatened with an auto-da-fé, he agreed to share her with the Grand Inquisitor; now he has her on Mondays, Wednesdays and the Sabbath, and the Inquisitor has her on the other days.

She describes her invitation to the auto-da-fé, where the ladies were served with refreshments between the mass and the execution. She was amazed to see Pangloss and Candide (though she appreciated *his* white skin even more than the Captain's). She realised that Pangloss had cruelly deceived her, in claiming that all was for the best. She recalled all her sufferings, but above all the kiss behind the screen that caused them, and, praising God, sent the old woman to bring Candide here. She now offers him some supper, when Don Issachar arrives.

NOTES AND GLOSSARY:

Sabbath: the Sabbath is the seventh day of the week, the day of rest. The Jewish Sabbath began on Saturday, the Christian one on Sunday, hence the quarrel

immorality: the variety of Cunégonde's lovers emphasises the immorality of people from every class, country and religion

the Inquisitor: the auto-da-fé was not just an absurdly superstitious way of preventing another earthquake. The Inquisitor has another motive, probably his real one — to frighten his Jewish rival away from Cunégonde

---

Chapter 9

What became of Cunégonde, Candide, the Grand Inquisitor and a Jew.

The furious Jew, believing Candide to be a defenceless rival, draws a dagger. However, Candide has a sword, and kills him. The Grand Inquisitor now arrives. Candide realises the danger of another auto-da-fé; he sees a rival before him; and anyway he has already killed once. So he runs him through.

The old woman advises a prompt escape, especially as it is a pleasant night. The police discover the corpses and bury the Inquisitor in a beautiful Church, and throw Don Issachar on to the dung-heap.

By now, the fugitives are at an inn at Avacena in the Sierra Morena.

NOTES AND GLOSSARY:

Issachar: the Babylonian captivity of the Jews is described in the Old Testament. Therefore, Voltaire, in making Issachar so excessively angry, parodies Pangloss's use of superlatives, as he does frequently elsewhere in the novel.

police: the 'Sainte Hermandad', the holy brotherhood, was the medieval Spanish police force. By placing it in Portugal, Voltaire underlines the primitive nature of the Inquisition.

Chapter 10

The distress of Candide, Cunégonde and the old woman on reaching Cadiz, and their embarkation.

Their money and diamonds are stolen during the night. Cunégonde wonders where she will find another Jew or Inquisitor to replace them. They suspect that the thief was a monk. If everything on earth should be shared, laments Candide, then the monk should have left them at least something, in accordance with his own principles. A Benedictine monk buys a horse from them at a bargain price, and they continue their journey through Spain.

At Cadiz a fleet is preparing to take troops to fight the Jesuits, who have revolted in the colony of Paraguay against the Kings of Spain and Portugal. Candide's military experience earns him the rank of Captain.

They set sail for the New World. Candide hopes to find it the best of all possible worlds, for the old one of Europe has given them enough cause 'to groan a little'. Cunégonde is very pessimistic, after all her experiences. Yet, says the old woman, Cunégonde's misfortunes do not compare with her own.

NOTES AND GLOSSARY:

friar . . . prior: Voltaire satirises the morals of monks, who should renounce worldly goods. Here one steals (and we wonder why he came twice into Cunégonde's bedroom!) and another profits from their misery to drive a hard bargain over the horse

theft: Candide's view that 'worldly goods are common to all men' reflects that of Rousseau, whom Voltaire found impractical and naïve. It becomes an excuse for theft

voyage: the towns on the journey are real, but their route zigzags all over Spain, adding to the effect of a cartoon

Jesuit missionaries: the revolt in Paraguay really happened. Spain wished to transfer St Sacrament to Portugal, but her Jesuit missionaries resisted, electing their own king. Voltaire always distrusted Jesuits, so he assumed— perhaps unfairly—that the priests wanted to profit from the natives as Spain, the colonial power, already had. Candide's adventures emphasise that there is slavery and war in America. He will find the New World just as bad as the Old.

Chapter 11

The old woman's tale.

The ugly old woman turns out to be the daughter of Pope Urban X and of the Princess of Palestrina. She grew up in luxury: any of her dresses was worth more than all Westphalia! Her ladies-in-waiting gasped when they undressed her, the men longed to be in their place, and poets wrote mediocre verse about her beauty.

She fell passionately in love with the Prince of Massa-Carrara; his former mistress poisoned him and he died in convulsions—'but that's a mere trifle'.

She and her mother left on a holiday, but Moroccan pirates seized them. Like the Knights of Malta, they searched the women all over for diamonds 'with admirable diligence'. The negro captain ravished her— 'but such things are too commonplace to be worth discussing'.

The Emperor of Morocco's fifty sons were fighting fifty civil wars, when she arrived. Now they all fought to win her and her followers. They had vitriol in their veins, and ripped the woman apart in their desire. She herself lay dying amid the carnage: yet here, and in many similar scenes, the Moroccans never failed to pray to Mahommed five times a day.

Fainting beside a stream, the Pope's daughter was aware of a white man on her, bewailing in Italian that he was a eunuch.

NOTES AND GLOSSARY:

Pope Urban X: again Voltaire mocks the immorality of the Church and the aristocracy. As Catholic priests cannot marry, the Pope of all men should not have a child! Voltaire changed the name from Clement VIII, a real Pope, to Urban X, and cheerfully wrote a footnote praising his own discretion!

universal corruption: Massa-Carrara and Gaeta are in Italy; Salé is in Morocco. The Maltese Knights of St John are an ancient order of chivalry. Mulei Ismael was Sultan till 1727. Wherever she goes the old woman sees the same inhuman behaviour from people who should protect the weak. Neither Moslems nor Christians practise what they claim to believe

'O che sciagura . . .':   Voltaire illustrates two more abuses: firstly piracy, which also helped the slave trade; and secondly, the castration of children so that the Church choirboys would keep their beautiful voices regardless of their personal unhappiness. Thus 'O che sciagura . . .' is Italian for: 'what a pity to be without testicles'

Chapter 12

Continuation of the old woman's misfortunes.

They recognised each other: he used to be the court muscian to her mother. Like thousands of children in Naples each year, he was castrated so that he could sing beautifully in the choir. Now he had just concluded a treaty on behalf of his 'Christian' country: it would supply the Muslim Emperor, Mulei Ismael, with guns to destroy the trade of other Christian countries.

The eunuch sold her to the dey (or governor) of Algiers as a slave. Both men died in a plague that was far worse than any earthquake. She was sold in Tunis, Tripoli, Alexandria, Smyrna, Constantinople and finally taken by a Turkish officer to the defence of Azov against the Russians.

The starving Turkish garrison decided to eat the women. However, an iman—or priest—persuaded them to eat only one buttock from each lady. Then the fort fell, the Russians arrived and a French doctor cured the women.

A Russian made her his gardener in Moscow till he fell from power. She escaped across Europe, often suicidal but more often wanting to live, caressing the serpent that devoured her, namely life itself.

Everywhere she has met people who hated their lives, but she has only known of twelve suicides. She bets Cunégonde that everyone else on board has often thought himself the world's most unhappy man.

NOTES AND GLOSSARY:

Morocco: Christian Portugal allied with Moslem Morocco in the War of the Spanish Succession (1701–14) against other Christian countries. Voltaire shows how self-interest comes before faith

plague . . . famine: these are two more disasters over which man has little control, again disproving Pangloss's theories

Azov: the 'janisseries' were Turkish soldiers under the command of the 'aga'. The Russians attacked Azov in 1695; as usual Voltaire alters the facts of history to suit his purposes. Like the Oreillons, the soldiers eat human flesh. Voltaire regarded this as less wicked than the original killing

put an end to their misery: Voltaire believed that most people prefer life to death, even when faced with misery. Robeck, who drowned himself, is an exception. *Candide* shows how life could at least become tolerable

Chapter 13

How Candide had to leave the fair Cunégonde and the old woman.

The Pope's daughter is proved right. Candide regrets that he cannot respectfully question some of the late Pangloss's views.

In Buenos Ayres, the Governor, Don Fernando d'Ibaraa y Figueora y Mascarenes y Lampourdos y Souza is as proud and pompous as his name. He is struck by Cunégonde's beauty, and Candide, though alarmed, cannot lie like Abraham in the Bible and pretend that she is his wife. Don Fernando proposes to Cunégonde, who asks for a quarter of an hour to consider!

The old woman reckons that 'misfortunes give one rights' and Cunégonde should accept him. What is more, the police have recovered the stolen jewels and traced Cunégonde and Candide to America; she is penniless and Fernando will protect her, but Candide must flee.

NOTES AND GLOSSARY:

Buenos Ayres: this city, now the capital of Argentina, is on the south-east coast of South America

Don Fernando . . . : The Governor's absurd name parodies the vanity of the Spanish nobility

the ancients: Candide is too pure to lie, whereas Abraham pretended his wife Sarah was his sister, and Isaac did likewise with Rebecca. Voltaire enjoyed mocking the morality of the Old Testament

Chapter 14

How Candide and Cacambo were received by the Jesuits in Paraguay.

Cacambo, Candide's colourful valet, is a practical man. He bids Candide hurry, advises him to join the Jesuit army now—'it's a pleasure to do something different!'

Cacambo describes the system of the Jesuit fathers as 'a masterpiece of reason and justice': they take everything and give the Paraguayans nothing; they are priests to the kings of Spain and Portugal in Europe, yet here they wage war on them.

The Jesuit guards surround them, disarm them, and say all Spaniards must leave the country within three hours. Meanwhile the Reverend Father Provincial is on parade after saying mass. However, when the Reverend Commandant hears the news that Candide is German, he summons him gladly to his exotic bower. They eat a splendid meal from golden plates, whilst outside in the blazing sun the Paraguayans eat maize from wooden bowls.

Candide explains he is from 'the dirty province of Westphalia'. With tears of joy he recognises Cunégonde's brother, who embraces him. 'How happy Pangloss would have been if he had not been hanged!' cries Candide, and reveals that Cunégonde is still alive.

NOTES AND GLOSSARY:

Cacambo:	his name suggests 'caca', a child's word for excrement. The cheerful, down-to-earth servant plays a traditional part in the romantic novel
reverend fathers:	Voltaire satirises the Jesuit's abuse of the natives
St Ignatius:	St Ignatius of Loyola (1491–1556) founded the order in 1534. As missionaries they should have been helping the Paraguayans. Voltaire finds a religious war particularly repulsive, and the mixture of religious and military ranks of 'los Padres', the Fathers, he considers a contradiction in terms

Chapter 15

How Candide killed his dear Cunégonde's brother.

The Commandant recalls the slaughter at Thunder-ten-tronckh. A Jesuit priest sprinkled his 'corpse' with holy water and made him blink. He revived and Father Croust, who felt 'the most tender friendship' for the handsome young man, sent him to Rome. From there the Jesuits sent him to Paraguay, where he is now a colonel and a priest and intends to excommunicate and defeat the Spanish troops.

He and his 'brother' Candide will rescue Cunégonde, he says. Candide gladly agrees, for he wants to marry her. The Baron is shocked at his insolent pretentions, for Candide has only seventy-one quarters of nobility. Candide firmly points out that Pangloss said that all men are equal and he means to marry her. The Baron strikes him with the flat of his sword, and Candide kills him. He cries 'I'm the best man in the world and I've already killed three men, and two of them were priests.'

Cacambo quickly disguises Candide in the Baron's robes and they gallop away.

NOTES AND GLOSSARY:

Croust:	he was a homosexual priest whom Voltaire met in Colmar in 1754. Thus Voltaire attacks both his enemy and the morals of the clergy in general
vineyard:	the baron is chosen to 'work in the vineyard', an image from St Matthew and St Luke that means to spread the gospel

reunions: The reappearance of characters to tell their stories is a tradition of the picaresque novel. Voltaire parodies it, for his characters 'die' first. Disguise is another typical feature

---

Chapter 16

What happened to the two travellers with two girls, two monkeys and the savages known as Oreillons.

Resting in a meadow, Candide tells Cacambo he is too sad to eat—which does not stop him eating. They hear the cries of two naked girls, whose backsides two monkeys are nipping as they lightly run along. Candide shoots the monkeys. He is confident of the ladies' gratitude and glad to atone for the other killings.

Cacambo startles Candide yet again by pointing out that the monkeys were the girls' lovers. After all, they are one-quarter human, as he is one-quarter Spanish! They escape into a wood, and sleep. On waking they find themselves tied up and surrounded by fifty Oreillons, long-eared savages who intend to 'eat Jesuit'. Candide is distressed at this example of 'pure Nature' but Cacambo keeps cool. He argues that 'the laws of nature teach us to kill our neighbour' and that if you are hungry it is wiser to eat your enemy than to leave his body to the ravens. However, he explains that they share a common enemy and have just killed the Jesuit commandant. When this is confirmed, they are released amid scenes of joy. All of which reassures Candide that 'pure Nature is good' after all!

NOTES AND GLOSSARY:

Jesuit periodicals: with gentle irony, Voltaire suggests that the hungry Candide can still eat, so is not as desperate as he pretends. By making a reference to the Jesuit Trévoux Journal, Voltaire sarcastically implies that its criticism is more alarming than a killer's remorse or a lover's agony!

monkeys: the ladies have followed Rousseau's advice and gone right back to nature. Voltaire's monkeys ridicule the idea of the 'noble savage', though he shows elsewhere that 'civilised' man can hardly be said to behave any better

Oreillons: they have long ears because of the heavy ear-rings they wear. Cacambo convinces them, not by Christian arguments against killing, but by appealing to their friendship

Chapter 17

Arrival of Candide and Cacambo in the land of Eldorado and what they saw there.

Candide cannot bear to go far from Cunégonde, so they make for Cayenne in French Guiana. Terrible obstacles confront them, and eventually Cacambo suggests they drift downstream in their boat—they may not find something pleasant, but at least it will be different.

After a variety of scenery they disappear beneath a fearsome arch of rocks, their boat disintegrates on the reefs, but at last they reach a vast area ringed by inaccessible mountains. Everything is both beautiful and useful. Graceful people pass along the splendid roads in carriages drawn by llamas—'red sheep'—faster than horses.

Some children in golden rags drop the jewels they have been playing with, and their teacher smiles in surprise when Candide hands them to him. Even Cacambo is intrigued when the inn-keeper, after serving them an exotic meal, refuses all payment, especially the golden 'pebbles' from the road.

Candide feels that there must be an ideal state, and Eldorado may well be it; and he realises now that Pangloss was wrong about Westphalia.

NOTES AND GLOSSARY:

Eldorado: Voltaire's Eldorado—'the golden one' in Spanish —is based on the Inca Kingdom in Peru, where gold was plentiful. It symbolises the ideal state that man's reason should aim at, even if Candide's garden proves to be a more realistic goal. The dangers of the journey, in the tradition of the romantic story, emphasise the remoteness of the ideal

Chapter 18

What they saw in the land of Eldorado.

An old man of 172, in his simple dwelling—the door is 'only silver'—explains that Eldorado was once the Kingdom of the Incas. After the Spanish destroyed most of them in their search for golden 'mud', the rest vowed never to leave their country. Thus they have remained innocent and happy. Their religion is continually to thank the one God to whom they owe everything, and to sing hymns of praise. They would be mad to have 'monks that burn people who disagree with them'.

In a magnificent palace Candide and Cacambo are received by lovely girls and led by the officers to the King. They expect to have to grovel before him, but they are told to kiss him and he receives them most graciously.

They are shown the splendid public buildings, the fountains of sweet liquids and the palace of science; there are no courts, prisons or parliament.

Candide admits it is all far better than Westphalia, but wishes to return to Cunégonde, laden with treasure. Thus 'the two happy men resolved not to be so any longer'. The King respects their freedom, though he thinks that if one is 'reasonably well satisfied' with a place, one should stay. A brilliant contraption is devised to lift them and their 'valuables' above the mountains, and Candide plans to find Cunégonde and buy a kingdom.

NOTES AND GLOSSARY:

The old man: Voltaire respects the experience of old age

The Spaniards had a confused knowledge . . .: Voltaire took many historical details from a Spanish book by Garcilasso de la Vega (1535–1616), and from the expedition of the English explorer, Sir Walter Raleigh (1552–1618), in 1595. Spanish greed for gold destroyed the Incas. On these facts Voltaire builds a fairy-tale world where all really is 'for the best'; natural disasters do not seem to happen in Eldorado, so to this extent Voltaire's ideal remains unattainable. However, he shows the human qualities he admires most: good taste, gratitude, generosity, moderation, a scientific approach to problems and above all tolerance

gratitude: Voltaire's deism emerges here. Men should thank God for their lives—elsewhere he emphasises that God is not concerned with individuals, but here he concentrates on the positive side of God's creation

Law Courts: Eldorado is a just society based on human reason. It does not need churches, prisons or law-courts. Voltaire knows that real life could never be so simple, but the vision shows Pangloss's theories in their true light

Chapter 19

What happened to them in Surinam and how Candide met Martin.

After their initial elation, Candide and Cacambo lose llama after llama, until only two remain. Candide realises that 'the riches of this world are transitory'; only his virtue and his vision of Cunégonde remain.

In Surinam, in Dutch Guiana, he sees the slave of the merchant Mr Vanderdendur. The negro works in the sugar plantations. They cut off his hand rather than stop the mill when his finger was trapped; and they cut off his leg to stop him running away—'that is what it costs for you to eat sugar in Europe'. His parents sold him to the slave traders, and though the Dutch 'fetishes'—or priests—preach that we are all the children of Adam, it seems a horrible way to treat one's relations. Candide weeps and renounces optimism, 'that mania for claiming that all is well when things are bad'.

Shocked to learn that Cunégonde is Don Fernando's mistress, he sends Cacambo to Buenos Ayres to buy her back, and arranges to meet them in Venice.

Vanderdendur agrees to sail to Italy, but vanishes with the llamas. A Dutch judge calmly pockets more money and is no help. Candide despairs at the wickedness of mankind. He decides to sail for Bordeaux with the most miserable man he can find. From a huge number of applicants he chooses Martin, whose family have abused him, who is persecuted as a Socinian, and who had the supreme misfortune to work for Dutch publishers. The other candidates think it a very unfair choice!

NOTES AND GLOSSARY:

Vanderdendur:	many French towns owed their prosperity to the heartless slave-trade, which was still flourishing in 1758. Vanderdendur's name is a combination of Vanderussen, a magistrate, and Vandurea, a bookseller, both of whom Voltaire disliked; the name means appropriately 'of the hard tooth'. Voltaire violently criticises the religious hypocrisy of this cruel profiteer
judge:	whereas the Dutch judge is as avaricious as his compatriot Vanderdendur, the Spaniard is satirised for his cowardice
persecuted:	Martin is wrongly suspected of being a disciple of Socini, a Siennese reformer of the sixteenth century, who denied the Trinity and the divinity of Christ

Chapter 20

What happened at sea to Candide and Martin.

During their voyage Candide and Martin discuss philosophy, and though it does not get them anywhere, at least it consoles them to be able to talk. After a meal, and thinking of Cunégonde, Candide tends towards Pangloss's theories. Martin, however, is a Manichean, and believes God has abandoned this world, this 'globule', to the Devil (except in Eldorado); everywhere he sees envy, murder and sorrow.

They witness a battle, in which Vanderdendur's boat is sunk. Candide is overjoyed to recover a llama and says God has punished the Dutch villain. Martin replies that the Devil drowned the passengers. The return of the llama encourages Candide to hope that he will find Cunégonde again.

NOTES AND GLOSSARY:

forces of evil: not surprisingly they do not go by the Cape of Good Hope, for Martin has none and Candide is very depressed! The Manichean believes that men are in the power of an evil force and cannot improve. Candide, like many people, including Voltaire, does not rule out all hope

philosophy: Candide and Martin enjoy their discussions. Voltaire recognises the pleasure one can derive from philosophy—after all, *Candide* is a philosophical novel. He only objects when the ideas are clearly absurd or, more important still, when there is work to be done

Chapter 21

Candide and Martin's discussion as they approach the coast of France.

In sight of France, Martin discusses the main occupation of the inhabitants—love, scandal and talking nonsense. In Paris a chaotic mob seek non-existent pleasure. He himself was robbed and imprisoned there, and met a rabble of writers, intriguers and religious fanatics.

Candide prefers to hurry to Italy to see Cunégonde, and Martin agrees as Venice is expensive and only Candide has any money. He thinks that the theory that the earth was once a sea is mere fantasy; the earth was created to make men mad! Candide lists all mankind's vices and wonders if men have always massacred each other. Martin is sure of it, for it is as natural as a hawk killing pigeons. Candide is still defending free will when they reach Bordeaux.

NOTES AND GLOSSARY:

Paris: Martin's Paris contrasts utterly with Eldorado. When Candide asks if men have 'always' done evil, he implies that he now accepts much of Martin's picture of mankind. Yet he clings to the idea of 'free will', which offers a chance of improvement. Voltaire interrupts him, suggesting men will always argue about this

delirious ravings:	Voltaire disliked the Jansenists' religion, shared by his own brother, which preached salvation for a select few. When they went into trances and convulsions, he thought they were indulging in superstitious nonsense. Their sect was founded by Cornelius Jansen (1585–1638), Bishop of Ypres. Their influence in France declined around 1730

Chapter 22

What happened to Candide and Martin in France.

Candide leaves the llama to the Bordeaux Academy of Science, where a scholar proves mathematically why its wool is red. His money attracts many 'friends', as he joins the throng to Paris. His doctors make his illness worse. He rejects a religious 'certificate to heaven'.

An 'obliging' priest from Périgord takes Martin and Candide to the theatre. Though Candide is moved, a critic condemns the play, partly because the author cannot speak Arabic and does not believe in Descartes' theory of innate ideas. He reckons only sixteen or so plays out of some six thousand are of any value—which Martin finds surprisingly many.

Candide is shocked that the actresses who play the part of Queens on stage are thrown on to the dung-hill when they die. He asks what the 'pig' does, who condemned the play, and learns he is a poisonous snake of a critic who hates literary success as eunuchs hate pleasure.

He loses a fortune at the card tables of the Marquise de Parolignac (Marchioness of Doubletakesworthy). At supper scorn is poured on Gauchat and Trublet, two theologians. However, a 'man of good taste' sensibly discusses tragedy, showing it must be sublime but above all seem natural. He rejects Pangloss's ideas, for life seems to him an 'eternal war', and Martin sees the shadows in the 'beautiful picture of life' as 'horrible stains'.

The Marchioness uses her feminine wiles to obtain two diamonds, and Candide regrets he has been unfaithful to Cunégonde. The priest learns that he is awaiting a letter from her, and next day one comes, informing Candide that she is ill in Paris! He rushes to the bedside in the darkened room; she cannot speak, but a plump hand accepts his money! The police, summoned by the treacherous priest, arrest him, but he bribes them. And though foreigners are in danger after an attempt on Louis XV's life, they escape from Normandy and take a ship for Portsmouth. Candide feels he has been saved from hell.

NOTES AND GLOSSARY:
Paris: the two longest scenes in the book are Eldorado and

Paris, and they balance each other artistically and morally. One is an earthly paradise, the other hell on earth. The vices of the big city make nonsense of Pangloss's theories. Voltaire aims here at his personal enemies rather than at the world in general. Although a sense of man's wickedness clearly emerges, this chapter has therefore inevitably dated more than most of the book

Bordeaux Academy: the essay prize satirises Maupertuis, Voltaire's rival in Berlin, who tended to express his ideas in glib mathematical formulae

note from his confessor: a dying Jansenist wanting the last rites needed a certificate to prove that he agreed with a Papal decree against the Jansenists! The system inevitably caused bribery and bitterness

innate ideas: René Descartes (1596-1650), wrote *Discourse on Method* (1637), expounding the dualism of the mind and the body

a new tragedy . . . : the play Candide admires is Voltaire's *Tancrède*, a story of Norman knights and Moors, which has an original atmosphere and verse-form. Mlle Clairon played the lead in it. The 'man of taste' defends Voltaire against contemporary critics such as Elie Fréron (1718-76).

Monimia: actresses were excommunicated from the Church. Thus Voltaire's friend Adrienne Lecouvreur, who played Monime in his *Mithridate*, was refused a Christian burial, to Voltaire's disgust

cheating: cheating at cards was commonplace, for they were played for high stakes. Voltaire and Mme du Châtelet had to flee to Sceaux, when he claimed that she had been cheated at the table of the Queen herself. In the game of faro a player could double his stake if he won. To show this he bent the corner of his card, a 'paroli', from which the Marquise de Parolignac takes her dubious title; after a second win, the player could again bend the card, a 'sept-et-le-va de campagne'. Cheats bent their cards even when they had lost

Molinists: the Molinists, who opposed the Jansenists, followed the ideas on free will of the Spanish Jesuit Luis Molina (1535-1600)

beggar from Artois: Jean Châtel in 1594 tried to kill King Henri IV, and in 1610 François Ravaillac (1578-1610), succeeded.

In 1757 Robert François Damiens (1714–57), from
Artois, tried to kill Louis XV. Voltaire fears such
religious fanatics, whose intolerance drives them
to murder

Chapter 23

Candide and Martin go to the coast of England, and what they see there.

Martin considers the English mad in a melancholy way. They are
fighting France for some snowy land in Canada worth less than the war
itself. He and Candide watch the execution of Admiral Byng for being
too far from his enemy in a battle; but Candide points out that the
French Admiral must have been just as far from Byng. He learns that
the English like to kill an occasional admiral 'to encourage the others'.
Shocked, Candide is prepared to risk another Dutch ship to take him
straight to Venice. At the prospect of seeing Cunégonde again, he cries
that all is for the best.

NOTES AND GLOSSARY:

what devil is it that rules the roost . . .?: again Voltaire condemns the
waste of human life. He had tried to save Byng. He
finds all war wicked, and this one particularly
pointless. He satirises the coldness of the English
character with its ceremonial execution and cynical
warning to other Admirals

Chapter 24

Concerning Paquette and Brother Giroflée.

Unable to find Cacambo anywhere in Venice, Candide curses Europe
and regrets Eldorado. Martin is sure Cacambo will not turn up. They
see a vigorous young monk and his loving girl-friend, and bet as to
whether or not they are really happy.

At supper Martin wins his bet. The girl reveals herself to be Paquette.
A Franciscan monk seduced her; she was thrown out of the Baron's
castle; a doctor kept her until he gave his wife poison to 'cure her cold'
and Paquette went to prison. The judge made her his mistress, and she
became a prostitute—a life of misery, which will end on the dung-hill.
Her friend, Brother Giroflée, also curses his fate. His monastery is full
of hatred. He was forced to join it at fifteen so that his elder brother
would receive a bigger inheritance, and he is tempted to become a
Moslem.

Martin, from his experience of life, doubts if Cunégonde will make

Candide happy. He sees little difference in the sorrows of the Doge of Venice and those of the gondoliers. He would like to meet Senator Pococurante, who has 'never known sorrow'.

NOTES AND GLOSSARY:

Paquette and Giroflée: two more evils undermine Candide's faith in Pangloss. Paquette realistically describes a prostitute's fate. Giroflée, a Theatin monk from a sixteenth-century foundation in Rome, suffers the fate of many younger sons. Their parents wanted to keep their money in one family, so they left it all to their eldest son, and the penniless second son had to enter a monastery

Pococurante: the Doge is the ruler of Venice. The gondoliers ferry passengers along the canals. To Martin rich and poor are more or less equally unhappy. Pococurante, who lives on the river Brenta, has a character suggested by his Italian name—'cares little'

Chapter 25

Visit to Count Pococurante, a Venetian nobleman.

In his magnificent palace on the Brenta, Pococurante, a very rich man of sixty, receives Candide and Martin with polite indifference. He is bored by his lovely serving girls. He likes only naturalistic paintings and so rejects his Raphaels. Modern French music he finds difficult and tiring, and opera has become a monstrous mixture of bad tragedy, silly songs and effeminate heroes.

Candide asks his views on the authors of the splendidly bound volumes in his library. He is told that Homer's *Odyssey* is a boring repetition of identical battles, obligatory in every library as an ancient monument, but as useless as a rusty medal. Most of Virgil's *Aeneid* is cold and unpleasant. Apart from a few helpful maxims, Horace's *Satires* and *Odes* are tasteless. Cicero merely admits to his own ignorance. The Academy of Science produces only theories and no practical inventions. Most plays and sermons are worthless. Italian writers say only what is permitted by the Dominican monks, and the English, though more liberal, are corrupted by party politics. Milton's *Paradise Lost* is an 'obscure, bizarre and disgusting' picture of the Creation. Even his lovely garden seems tasteless to Pococurante.

He despises fools who admire everything in a famous writer. He is concerned only with his own opinions. Candide admires his attitude.

NOTES AND GLOSSARY:

tired: Pococurante is bored. Voltaire shows that even very rich people may not be happy. Since they never need to work they do not know the humble satisfaction that Candide eventually gains from his gardening

Raphael: Raphael Sanzio (1483-1520). Italian painter, many of whose masterpieces were commissioned for the Vatican

Homer: (*c.* ninth century BC). Supposed Ionian poet whose *Iliad* and *Odyssey* are epics that symbolise Hellenistic unity, relating the exploits of gods and men in the Trojan War

Virgil: Publius Vergilius Maro (70-19BC). His epic poem *The Aeneid* celebrates the foundation of Rome by Aeneas of Troy and the Roman unification of the world under Augustus Caesar (63 BC–AD 14)

Horace: Quintus Horatius Flaccus (65-8BC). Roman poet whose *Odes, Epistles* and *Satires* extol the virtues of moderation and simplicity

Cicero: Marcus Tullius Cicero (106-43 BC). Roman orator and politician

Milton: John Milton (1608-74). English poet, whose epics *Paradise Lost* (1667) and *Paradise Regained* (1671) depict the conflict of good and evil

Pococurante's judgement: several of Pococurante's views on the arts are in fact Voltaire's. Both admire realism, simplicity and usefulness. Many critics disagree with Pococurante's judgements, particularly on the Greek and Latin classics and on Milton's seventeenth century English epic, *Paradise Lost*. However, Voltaire emphasises through the Senator that what really matters is to have your own opinions, whatever other people say

In Italy . . . : Pococurante despises the Italians, with their great history, for not daring to speak out against the Jacobins, a Dominican order of the Catholic Church. The English, though democratic, annoy him because they write only in defence of the Whig party, or the Tory one, which Voltaire's friend Bolingbroke had led

Chapter 26

Concerning a supper that Candide and Martin took with six strangers and who they were.

In his hotel Candide joyfully meets Cacambo, who is now the slave of one of the six other guests. He says Cunégonde is in Constantinople and they must leave after supper. Each stranger is addressed as 'Your Majesty', and the sixth is warned by his servant that they may both be locked up for debt. Candide thinks it is a carnival joke, but in fact they are all kings in Venice for the festivities: Sultan Achmet III, dethroned by his nephew; Emperor Ivan of Russia, dethroned in the cradle; Charles Edward Stuart, whose followers were executed when he tried to regain the British throne for his family; Augustus III, the King of Poland and Elector of Saxony, defeated by Frederick the Great; Stanislas Leczinski, who lost the Polish throne, but was given the Duchy of Lorraine, which he ruled well; and Theodore, who was King of Corsica, but went to prison in London and fears the same fate here. The other kings give Theodore twenty gold sequins each, but Candide gives two thousand and a diamond. He says he is not a king, and does not want to be one. He does not even notice the arrival of four more Serene Highnesses, for he wants only to see Cunégonde.

NOTES AND GLOSSARY:

the supper: this meeting could never in fact have taken place, for Achmet died in 1736 before some of the kings lost their thrones. Even if it had been possible, it would remain incredible. In this brilliantly inventive scene, Voltaire again satirises the coincidences in a romantic novel. More seriously, he reminds Candide that nothing is certain in life. The politics and ambitions of others can overthrow even the greatest men. The kings 'submit to God's Providence', but Voltaire suggests that God is not at all interested in their fate

King of Poland: Voltaire often enjoyed Stanislas's hospitality at Lunéville in Lorraine. When he read *Candide*, the Duke said all the kings would have been welcome guests in his court, except for the adventurer Theodore! Like Candide, Voltaire himself had no desire for a title. When it was rumoured that he would be ennobled, he said 'Marquis Voltaire would be good for nothing but to show at the fair with the monkeys!'

Chapter 27

Candide's voyage to Constantinople.

Cacambo arranges their passage to Constantinople with 'his miserable Highness', Achmet. Candide is optimistic when he compares his fate to that of the kings. Martin is unimpressed by the 'honour' of eating with them.

Cacambo reveals that Cunégonde washes dishes for a penniless Hungarian refugee, Ragotski, and that she is now ugly. Candide says he will do his duty and love her always. He wonders if he is unhappier than the kings. Martin says no one can read men's hearts, but millions are worse off than the kings; and Candide tends to agree.

He buys Cacambo's freedom, and they sail in a galley up the Propontide Sea in search of Cunégonde. A Turk thrashes two convict oarsmen. Candide recognises the Baron's son and Pangloss! 'Is this the great philosopher?' asks Martin. Candide buys their freedom for fifty thousand sequins which he gets from a Jew for a diamond worth twice as much. Pangloss weeps with gratitude; the Baron nods and promises to return the money. They take another galley and continue their search for Cunégonde.

NOTES AND GLOSSARY:

Ragotski:	he lost a struggle for power with the Emperor Joseph II in the War of the Spanish Succession. Again Voltaire shows the brittle nature of glory
pirate:	the pirates took Cunégonde and Cacambo to Matapan, Milos, Nikaria and Samos in Greece; to Petra in Arabia; and up the Dardanelles, through the Sea of Marmora (the Propontide) to Scutari on the Bosphorus. Thus piracy devastates another large area of the world. The 'levantis', or Turkish soldiers, on the galley, recall the theme of slavery
picaresque:	again Voltaire parodies the romantic adventure story with the tearful reunion, the coincidences, the mercenary Jews, the oriental setting, and the hasty flight to the beloved Cunégonde

Chapter 28

What happened to Candide, Cunégonde, Pangloss, Martin, etc.

Candide apologises to the Baron's son for thrusting his sword through him; the Baron's son admits that he himself acted hastily. He says how, after being cured, he was sent to Constantinople as chaplain to the French ambassador. He went bathing in the nude with the Sultan's page boy, for which—most unjustly, he feels—he was beaten and sent to the galleys.

Pangloss says that the rain prevented the fire at the auto-da-fé, so they hanged him with a wet rope that did not work. A surgeon wished to dissect his 'corpse', and he cried out so loud that his wife thought the Devil was in the heretic's body! A barber stitched him up, and he became a servant of a Knight of Malta, then of a Venetian merchant in Constantinople. At a mosque a girl with bare breasts dropped her flowers; Pangloss lingeringly returned them, which annoyed the priest, and he too was beaten and sent to the galleys. He was put beside the Baron's son. The other prisoners told them this was all perfectly commonplace.

Candide asks Pangloss if in his misery he still thought all was for the best. He says he still does, for it is not 'seemly' for a philosopher to change his mind. He still believes in the theories of pre-established harmony, of the plenum and of subtle matter, for 'Leibniz cannot be wrong'.

NOTES AND GLOSSARY:

I still hold my original views: Pangloss clings to Wolff's interpretation of Leibniz's theories. So he continues to believe in the 'pre-established harmony' of the body and soul, which God causes to act together. He believes that the universe is a 'plenum', a fullness, and therefore outer-space cannot exist. He believes also that heavenly bodies move in a 'subtle matter', a jelly-like substance that keeps them in position. Voltaire agreed with Newton's dismissal of these ideas. Above all, he satirises the philosophical jargon and the obstinate vanity of philosophers who will not admit they are wrong even when they know it

Chapter 29

How Candide found Cunégonde and the old woman again.

Still philosophising, they all arrive at the Prince of Transylvania's house. They find Cunégonde and the old woman hanging out the washing. Cunégonde is ugly, blood-shot and wrinkled. The Baron grows pale. Candide staggers back in horror, but recovers politely, and buys the women's freedom.

Cunégonde, unaware she is now ugly, insists that Candide should marry her, and he dares not refuse. The Baron forbids the marriage, as their children would not be noble enough. Candide angrily points out all his own kindness and threatens to 'kill him again'. The Baron says he can kill him again, but 'you won't marry my sister while I'm alive'.

NOTES AND GLOSSARY:

discussion: they still 'discussed' and 'argued'. Voltaire suggests that man will never agree on the solution to philosophical problems. It is more useful to work instead. 'Contingent events' are those that happen by chance, as opposed to those that are predetermined

Cunégonde: her beauty has symbolised Candide's ideal of happiness all through the book. Her ugliness shatters his unrealistic hopes of perfection. Yet later she proves a useful member of society. Candide will learn to modify his ambitions and to make the best of things

Chapter 30

Conclusion.

Candide no longer really wants to marry Cunégonde. However, her insistence and the Baron's impertinence spur him on. He sends the Baron back to Rome in the next galley, and thus enjoys catching a Jesuit and punishing a German baron's pride at the same time.

On their little farm, they are all desperately bored. Only Martin patiently accepts that man is born to live 'in the restlessness of anxiety or the lethargy of boredom'. They philosophise when they see boatloads of exiled Turkish officers. Paquette and Giroflée turn up, penniless again; she is still a prostitute and he has become a Moslem.

A dervish tells them not to meddle in philosophical questions which are beyond them; he compares men to the mice on board the Sultan's boat. His advice on life is to 'be quiet'. He slams the door on Pangloss.

An old man is not interested in the name of the Mufti who has just been strangled; he is very happy in his own little house. He entertains them splendidly, and says hard work drives away the three great evils — boredom, vice and need.

Candide prefers the old man's life to that of the six kings. This makes Pangloss list many biblical and historical kings who fell from glory. Candide interrupts to say 'we must cultivate our garden'. Pangloss agrees, for man was put into the Garden of Eden to work. Martin says that the only tolerable way of life is to work without arguing.

The farm prospers and they all develop their talents. Pangloss some-times reflects on the chain of events in this 'best of all possible worlds'; if Candide had not been kicked out of the castle, had not been tortured by the Inquisition, had not crossed America, had not killed the Baron, and had not lost his llamas, they would not now be eating lemons and pistachios. But Candide politely repeats that 'we must go and work in the garden'.

NOTES AND GLOSSARY:

the Baron's intransigence . . . retract: Candide's motives for marrying are based on a mixture of stubbornness, pride and charity; experience has taught him to compromise even his most cherished ideals

attitudes: during the comic expulsion of the Baron and in their subsequent misery, all the characters once more illustrate their different philosophies of life

boredom: Martin says that life is alarming or boring. Their adventures have shown the alarming side; now they endure the tedium that destroyed Pococur-ante's pleasure

the dervish: he emphasises that God is not concerned with indi-vidual misfortunes. In slamming the door, he shows that he finds philosophy a waste of time

ministers: the 'catastrophic' fall of the ministers causes a sensation 'for some hours'. The anti-climax recalls that glory is ephemeral, and that people soon forget each other's problems

old man: 'boredom, vice and poverty' neatly summarise the misery Candide has seen. The good old man offers him a healthy philosophy: hard work brings con-tentment. Incidentally, the view from his Ferney estate over Lake Geneva reminded Voltaire of Constantinople

Pangloss: he airs his knowledge by quoting from the *Book of Kings* and the *Book of Judges* in the Bible, and from many historical tragedies. Any one of his examples throws doubt on his optimistic philos-ophy!

When man was placed . . .: Pangloss recalls Adam in the Garden of Eden, by quoting from the Bible, Genesis 2:15. Candide was thrown out of an 'earthly paradise'— as he used to think—in Westphalia. Now he has found, if not Eden, at least a worthwhile garden to cultivate and enjoy

Voltaire's philosophical conclusion: the dervish and the old man suggest that people should get on with their own lives and not worry about philosophy or politics in Constantinople. Yet Voltaire is obviously profoundly concerned with other peoples' misery, or he would not have written *Candide* or undertaken so many social reforms himself. What then does he mean by 'dig your garden'?

Above all, Candide has learnt to think realistically. Now Voltaire advises him to be equally practical in his actions. There is no point in attempting the impossible; the good old man knows that he personally could never influence Turkish politics. However, if you can do something constructive, whether on a world scale like Voltaire, or on a humble one in your own little community, then you should. Thus the last paragraph of *Candide* is a recipe for personal satisfaction *and* an appeal to help your fellow men. It does not advise you to cut yourself off selfishly from the world. It heralds the great battle cry, 'Crush the infamous'.

Part 3

Commentary

Candide is like the sugar-coated pill that a doctor gives to his patient. Because it is so funny, it maintains our interest in the profound moral issues that it raises. Effortlessly Voltaire diagnoses the diseases in society and offers his remedy of common sense and hard work.

The sense of justice that distinguishes his own life is felt in every page. Artistically too, every detail of the characterisation, the structure and the style heightens this essential mood. Even when the satire is most destructive, Voltaire still gives a message of hope: not the silly optimism of Pangloss, but real hope. Eldorado is no doubt too perfect to be possible, but with honesty, industry and luck people can still make life more bearable and more just.

Ideas

CHARACTERISATION: THE SATIRE OF A PHILOSOPHY

Each character helps Candide to find a sensible philosophy of life. He comes to distrust both Pangloss's empty optimism and Martin's deadly pessimism, for both of them are negative attitudes. After all, if life is perfect or hopeless, there is nothing one can do either way to improve it. All the other characters increase his experience of mankind; and from their behaviour he learns the need to be realistic and energetic.

Candide: innocence learning from experience

(1) He is totally trusting:

Sa physionomie annonçait son âme. Il avait le jugement assez droit, avec l'esprit le plus simple; (Chapter 1)

You could read his character in his face. He combined sound judgement with unaffected simplicity (p.19)

He naïvely accepts Pangloss's theories, as he is not really concentrating:

il croyait innocemment, car il trouvait Mlle. Cunégonde extrêmement belle. (Chapter 1)

he listened attentively and with implicit belief, for he found Lady Cunégonde extremely beautiful (p.20)

(2) Conscripted by the Bulgars, he is offered a choice between flogging and execution:

Il eut beau dire que les volontés sont libres, et qu'il ne voulait ni l'un ni l'autre, il fallut faire un choix. (Chapter 2)

It was useless to declare his belief in free will and say he wanted neither; he had to make his choice (p.24)

—already he is learning that our choice is usually not between good and bad, but between bad and worse.

(3) In the War:

il tremblait comme un philosophe (Chapter 3)

He trembled like a philosopher (p.25)

(4) The Dutch preacher dents his faith in human tolerance, but Jacques restores it:

Maître Pangloss me l'avait bien dit que tout est au mieux dans ce monde. (Chapter 3)

My tutor Pangloss was quite right when he told me that all is for the best in this world of ours (p.27)

(5) In the earthquake he cries:

Voici le dernier jour du monde! (Chapter 5)

The Day of Judgement has come! (p.32)

(6) The auto-da-fé reinforces his despair:

Epouvanté, interdit, éperdu, tout sanglant, tout palpitant, Candide se disait à lui-même: 'Si c'est ici le meilleur des mondes possibles, que sont donc les autres?' (Chapter 6)

The terrified Candide stood weltering in blood and trembling with fear and confusion. 'If this is the best of all possible worlds', he said to himself, 'What can the rest be like?' (p.37)

(7) Candide kills Don Issachar in self-defence, and now faces the jealous Inquisitor. He reasons:

Si ce saint homme appelle du secours, il me fera infailliblement brûler, il pourra en faire autant de Cunégonde; il m'a fait fouetter impitoyablement; il est mon rival; je suis en train de tuer; il n'y a pas à balancer. (Chapter 9)

If this holy man calls for help, he will assuredly have me burnt, and Cunégonde too, in all probability. I have been mercilessly whipped at his orders; besides he's my rival. I've got into the way of killing people. There's no time to hesitate. (p.45)

—thus Candide's passion and self-interest make him aware that people often of necessity have to make a choice of evils.

(8) The prospect of America renews his optimism:

C'est certainment le nouveau monde qui est le meilleur des univers possibles. (Chapter 10)

It is undoubtedly the new world that is the best of all possible universes. (p.48)

(9) His tears of sorrow on leaving Cunégonde turn to tears of joy on finding the Baron; soon he weeps again in total bewilderment, after having to 'kill' him:

Hélas . . . je suis le meilleur homme du monde, et voilà déjà trois hommes que je tue; et dans ces trois il y a deux prêtres! (Chapter 15)

God! . . . I am the best tempered man there ever was, yet I have already killed three men, and two of them were priests. (p.67)

(10) When the Oreillons do not eat him, he shows a naïve faith in primitive man's goodness:

la pure nature est bonne (Chapter 16)

There is a sterling goodness in unsophisticated nature. (p.72)

(11) In Eldorado, he reveals his growing scepticism:

Et quoi qu'en dît maître Pangloss, je me suis souvent aperçu que tout allait mal en Vestphalie. (Chapter 17)

And whatever Professor Pangloss might say, I often noticed that all went badly in Westphalia. (p.77)

(12) Even Eldorado does not satsify him, for Cunégonde still symbolises his ideal. His confidence returns:

. . . nous verrons ensuite quel royaume nous pourrons acheter. (Chapter 18)

We will then see what Kingdom we can buy. (p.84)

(13) Seeing the Surinam slave he rejects optimism:

'O Pangloss!' s'écria Candide, 'tu n'avais pas deviné cette abomination; c'en est fait, il faudra qu'à la fin je renonce à ton optimisme.— Qu'est-ce qu'optimisme? disait Cacambo.—Hélas! dit Candide, c'est la rage de soutenir que tout est bien quand on est mal.' (Chapter 19)

'Oh, Pangloss!' cried Candide. 'A scandal like this never occurred to you! But it's the truth, and I shall have to renounce that optimism of yours in the end.' 'What is optimism?' asked Cacambo. 'It's the passion for maintaining that all is right, when all goes wrong with us.' (p.86)

(14) He is further disillusioned by the Dutch captain and judge:

La méchanceté des hommes se présentait à son esprit dans toute sa laideur. (Chapter 19)

The wickedness of man appeared to him in all its ugliness. (p.89)

(15) In his discussion with Martin on board ship, he claims that there is some good in men. He still has faith in a Providence which punishes the wicked:

le crime est puni quelquefois; ce coquin de patron hollaindais a eu le sort qu'il méritait. (Chapter 20)

. . . crime is sometimes punished. That rogue of a Dutch captain has had the fate he deserved. (p.93)

—Martin ridicules the idea.

(16) Candide begins to reveal a much more realistic view of men:

Croyez-vous . . . qu'ils aient toujours été menteurs, fourbes, perfides, ingrats, brigands, faibles, volages, lâches, envieux, gourmands, ivrognes, avares, ambitieux, sanguinaires, calomniateurs, débauchés, fanatiques, hypocrites et sots? (Chapter 21)

Do you think that men . . . have always been false, cozening, faithless, ungrateful, thieving, weak, inconstant, mean-spirited, envious, greedy, drunken, miserly, ambitious, bloody, slanderous, debauched, fanatic, hypocritical and stupid? (p.96)

(17) In Paris, a sick society, symbolically he falls ill. He leaves for England, feeling:

être délivré de l'enfer (Chapter 22)

he had been delivered from hell (p.109)

(18) Shocked by Byng's fate, shuddering at the sight of Lisbon again, he still revives his optimism at the thought of Cunégonde:

Tout est bien, tout va bien, tout va le mieux qu'il soit possible. (Chapter 23)

All is well; we're on the right road now, and the outlook is as fine as possible. (p.111)

(19) Unable to find her he switches to black pessimism:

Que vous avez raison, mon cher Martin! tout n'est qu'illusion et calamité. (Chapter 24)

How right you are, my dear Martin! There is nothing here but illusion and one calamity after another. (p.112)

(20) He loses his bet about Paquette and Giroflée, which makes him more disillusioned than ever. However, he is impressed by Pococurante's distaste for everything:

n'y a-t-il pas du plaisir à tout critiquer? (Chapter 25)

isn't there a pleasure in criticising everything? (p.124)

—but Martin cynically rejects this:

'C'est-à-dire', reprit Martin, 'qu'il y a du plaisir à n'avoir pas de plaisir?' (Chapter 25)

'That is to say', said Martin, 'that there is a pleasure in not being pleased.' (p.124)

However, Candide still pins his faith on Cunégonde.

(21) He compares his situation to that of the dethroned Kings and, egoistically, is pleased:

Pour moi, je n'ai perdu que cent moutons, et je vole dans les bras de Cunégonde. Mon cher Martin, encore une fois, Pangloss avait raison, tout est bien. (Chapter 27)

For my part, I have lost nothing more than a hundred sheep, and I am hurrying to the arms of Cunégonde. I have been thinking it over again, my dear Martin, and find that Pangloss was quite right; all is for the best. (p.129)

(22) He asks Pangloss:

Quand vous avez été pendu, disséqué, roué de coups, et que vous avez ramé aux galères, avez-vous toujours pensé que tout allait le mieux du monde? (Chapter 28)

When you had been hanged, dissected and beaten unmercifully, and while you were rowing at your bench, did you still think that everything in this world is for the best? (p.136)

In challenging his teacher, Candide has clearly learned from his experiences.

(23) Bored and disillusioned by Cunégonde's ugliness, Candide suffers renewed doubts, but the good old man finally dispels them. Rejecting

the passive views of the optimist and the pessimist, he settles for a practical philosophy of hard work:

'Cela est bien dit', répondit Candide, 'mais il faut cultiver notre jardin.' (Chapter 30)

'That's true enough', said Candide, 'but we must first go and work in the garden.' (p.144)

Pangloss: thoughtless optimism

(1) He 'proves' that all is for the best:

Pangloss enseignait la métaphysico-théologo-cosmolo-nigologie. Il prouvait admirablement qu'il n'y a point d'effet sans cause, et que, dans ce meilleur des mondes possibles, le château de monseigneur le baron était le plus beau des châteaux, et madame la baronne la meilleure des baronnes possibles. (Chapter 1)

Pangloss taught metaphysico-theologo-cosmolo-nigology. He proved incontestably that there is no effect without a cause, and that in this best of all possible worlds, his lordship's country seat was the most beautiful of mansions and her ladyship the best of all possible ladyships. (p.20)

(2) His syphilitic appearance disproves his theories, just when Jacques' goodness has reassured Candide:

Un gueux tout couvert de pustules, les yeux morts, le bout du nez rongé, la bouche de travers, les dents noires, et parlant de la gorge, tourmenté d'une toux violente, et crachant une dent à chaque effort. (Chapter 3).

. . . a beggar covered in sores. His eyes were lifeless, the end of his nose had rotted away, his mouth was all askew, and his teeth were black. His voice was sepulchral, and a violent cough tormented him, at every bout of which he spat out a tooth. (p.27)

(3) To Jacques the symbolically one-eyed doctor takes optimism to its absurd logical extreme:

. . . les malheurs particuliers font le bien général; de sorte que plus il y a de malheurs particuliers, et plus tout est bien. (Chapter 4)

. . . private misfortunes contribute to the general good, so that the more private misfortunes there are, the more we find that all is well. (p.31)

By arguing that without syphilis they would have no chocolate, he takes the theory of cause and effect to absurdity. In the earthquake, he wastes time philosophising illogically while Candide begs for wine:

... car s'il y a un volcan à Lisbonne, il ne pouvait être ailleurs; car il
est impossible que les choses ne soient pas où elle sont; car tout est
bien. (Chapter 5)

... since if there is a volcano at Lisbon it could not be anywhere else.
For it is impossible for things not to be where they are, because everything is for the best. (p.35)

(5) Candide quotes the 'dead' Pangloss at the Marquise de Parolignac's,
saying evils are 'des ombres à un beau tableau'—('shadows in a beautiful picture'). Martin retorts:

... vos ombres sont des taches horribles (Chapter 22)

those shadows you speak of are horrible blemishes (p.124)

(6) After his rescue he is too vain to drop the jargon and admit he is
wrong:

Il ne me convient pas de me dédire, Leibnitz ne pouvant pas avoir
tort, et l'harmonie préétablie étant d'ailleurs la plus belle chose du
monde, aussi bien que la matière subtile (Chapter 28)

It would not be proper for me to recant, especially as Leibniz cannot
be wrong; and besides, the pre-established harmony, together with
the plenum and the materia subtilis, is the most beautiful thing in
the world. (p.136)

(7) Though bored, he still claims all is well. He philosophises on work
when others are working! He remains absurd to the end:

Tous les événements sont enchaînés dans le meilleur des mondes
possibles: car enfin si vous n'aviez pas été chassé d'un beau château
... vous ne mangeriez pas ici des cédrats confits et des pistaches.
(Chapter 30)

There is a chain of events in this best of all possible worlds; for if you
had not been turned out of a beautiful mansion ... you would not be
here eating candied fruit and pistachio nuts. (p.144)

Martin: total pessimism

(1) Chosen by Candide as a particularly unhappy man, the Manichean
sees only envy, hatred, murder and war, except in Eldorado:

... je vous avoue qu'en jetant la vue sur ce globe, ou plutot ce globule,
je pense que Dieu l'a abandonné à quelque être malfaisant. (Chapter
20)

... I confess that when I survey this globe, or rather this globule, I am forced to the conclusion that God has abandoned it to some mischievous power. (p.92)

(2) When the guilty Dutch captain drowns with his innocent passengers, Martin, who scoffs at the idea of Providence, says:

Dieu a puni ce fripon, le diable a noyé les autres (Chapter 20)

God has punished a scoundrel, but the devil has drowned the rest. (p.94)

—Voltaire would agree with this sarcasm, for Candide's idea that the wicked are punished belongs to a fairy-tale.

(3) The chaos of Paris confirms his view that the world exists: 'Pour nous faire enrager.' (To drive us mad.) Man is simply evil by nature:

si les éperviers ont toujours eu le même caractère, pourquoi voulez-vous que les hommes aient changé le leur? (Chapter 21)

if hawks have always had the same character, why should you suppose that men have changed theirs? (p.96)

(4) He sees through Giroflée's and Paquette's apparent happiness (Chapter 24), and realises that Pococurante is 'dégoûté de tout' (disgusted with everything) (Chapter 25). He cynically allows Candide to hope, but expects nothing really:

C'est toujours bien fait d'espérer (Chapter 25)

There's no harm in hoping (p.124)

(5) The fate of the six Kings confirms Martin's view that everything is liable to sudden doom, be it in the form of an earthquake, an assassination, a plague, a revolt, or whatever. Moreover, the Kings are not as badly off as most men:

Tout ce que je présume c'est qu'il y a des millions d'hommes sur la terre cent fois plus à plaindre que le roi Charles-Edouard, l'empereur Ivan, et le sultan Achmet. (Chapter 27)

All I can guess is that there are millions of men on earth with a hundred times more to complain of than King Charles Edward, Emperor Ivan and Sultan Achmet. (p.130)

(6) In Constantinople, typically, he advises throwing the Baron in the sea, for he approves of direct methods. He argues that man is:

né pour vivre dans les convulsions de l'inquiétude ou dans la léthargie de l'ennui. (Chapter 30)

born to suffer from the restlessness of anxiety or from the lethargy of boredom. (p.140)

He concludes:

Travaillons sans raisonner, . . . c'est le seul moyen de rendre la vie supportable. (Chapter 30)

We must work without arguing, . . . that is the only way to make life bearable. (p.144)

Cunégonde

(1) She is very attractive:

Cunégonde, âgée de dix-sept ans, était haute en couleur, fraîche, grasse, appétissante. (Chapter 1)

Cunégonde was a buxom girl of seventeen, with a fresh rosy complexion; altogether seductive. (p.19)

and she is eager for physical experiences after seeing Pangloss.

. . . retourna tout agitée, toute pensive, toute remplie du désir d'être savante, songeant qu'elle pourrait bien être la raison suffisante du jeune Candide, qui pouvait aussi être la sienne. (Chapter 1)

In a disturbed and thoughtful state of mind, she returned home filled with a desire for learning, and fancied she could reason equally well with young Candide and he with her. (p.21)

(2) Even when she recounts her terrible adventures, she betrays her sensuality:

Je vous dirai, avec vérité, que votre peau est encore plus blanche, et d'un incarnat plus parfait que celle de mon capitaine des Bulgares. (Chapter 8)

Your skin, I assure you, is much whiter than my Bulgar Captain's; it has a much more delicate bloom. (p.43)

(3) Robbed of her jewels, she again shows her amusingly self-centred attitude:

. . . où trouver des inquisiteurs et des juifs qui m'en donnent d'autres? (Chapter 10)

Where shall I find more Inquisitors and Jews to replace them? (p.46)

(4) When Don Fernando proposes marriage, she seizes her chance, regardless of Candide:

Cunégonde lui demanda un quart d'heure pour se recueillir (Chapter 13)

Cunégonde begged a quarter of an hour's grace to collect her thoughts. (p.59)

(5) Cunégonde, now very ugly, is still determined to profit from every situation:

elle fit souvenir Candide de ses promesses avec un ton si absolu que le bon Candide n'osa pas la refuser. (Chapter 29)

as she now reminded Candide of his promises with the utmost firmness, the good man did not dare to refuse her. (p.137)

(6) Her ugliness symbolises the end of Candide's empty dreams. However, she becomes a good pastry-cook, and finds pleasure in work.

The old woman

(1) She is very down-to-earth. Throughout her amazing adventures she repeats that she is a 'woman of experience' and still loves life in spite of everything:

Mais, passons; ce sont des choses si communes qu'elles ne valent pas la peine qu'on en parle. (Chapter 11)

But that's enough; such experiences are so common that they are not worth the trouble of describing. (p.51)

(2) The 'prudent' old woman puts profit before gratitude, and advises Cunégonde to marry Don Fernando at once:

les malheurs donnent des droits (Chapter 13)

misfortunes bring some privileges. (p.59)

(3) Her resilience is a good example for Candide, and not surprisingly she adapts well to her job as a laundress.

Cacambo

(1) His mixed ancestry and experience as chorister, verger, sailor, monk, commercial traveller, soldier and footman give him a cheerful, practical nature:

Quand on n'a pas son compte dans un monde, on le trouve dans un autre. C'est un très grand plaisir de voir et de faire des choses nouvelles (Chapter 14)

When you don't get what you expect on one side, you find it on the other. Fresh sights and fresh adventures are always welcome (p.62)

His quick wit saves Candide from the Oreillons and the Jesuits, and he is a loyal servant. From him Candide learns to be much more positive.

Jacques

(1) A realist, he recognises that life is not perfect:

> Il faut bien que les hommes aient un peu corrompu la nature, car ils ne sont pas nés loups et ils sont devenus loups. (Chapter 4)

> Men must have somewhat altered the course of Nature; for they were not born wolves, yet they have become wolves. (p.31)

In spite of his goodness, he dies; and the wicked sailor lives. From this, Candide learns that the good cannot rely on Providence to save them.

Pococurante

(1) He is bored despite his wealth:

> ... mais il n'y a dans tous ces livres que de vains systèmes, et pas une seule chose utile. (Chapter 25)

> but these collections merely consist of vain philosophical systems, devoid of any useful information. (p.121)

Candide learns that money is not enough to ensure happiness. Yet Pococurante also encourages him to trust his own judgement:

> Je ne lis que pour moi; je n'aime que ce qui est à mon usage. (Chapter 25)

> I read only to please myself, and enjoy only what suits my taste. (p.121)

The Baron's son

(1) He is 'in every way worthy of his father' (Chapter 1). His arrogance is 'neither of the Spanish nor the Jesuit kind' (Chapter 14), and his Germanic snobbery will not allow Candide to marry his sister. Though clearly a homosexual, he is full of righteous indignation at the 'injustice' of his punishment. Like the German philosopher Pangloss, the German aristocrat refuses to change even when Candide saves his life:

> Tu peux me tuer encore, dit le baron, mais tu n'épouseras pas ma soeur de mon vivant. (Chapter 29)

> 'You can kill me again if you like', said the Baron, 'but while I live you shall never marry my sister.' (p.138)

In calling him 'Maître fou' ('You unspeakable ass!'), Candide reveals a new independence.

Don Fernando

(1) His absurd name and behaviour reflect his Spanish arrogance:

> Il parlait aux hommes avec le dédain le plus noble, portant le nez si haut, élevant si impitoyablement la voix, prenant un ton si imposant, affectant une démarche si altière, que tous ceux qui le saluaient étaient tentés de le battre. (Chapter 13)

> He spoke to people with lordly contempt and with his nose in the air, and he harangued so loudly and unsparingly, assuming so impossible an attitude, and affecting such an arrogant bearing that everyone who saluted him wanted to hit him. (p.58)

He declares his passion for Cunégonde, yet sells her back to Cacambo for 'two million'. His egoism brings home to Candide the harshness of real life.

THE SATIRE OF RELIGION

Wherever Candide goes, 'always excepting Eldorado', he finds religious intolerance. Atrocities are committed in God's name. Voltaire condemns the churches whose behaviour makes nonsense of Pangloss's theories.

(1) The Dutch orator threatens Candide with prison for begging:

> '...je manque de pain.'—'Tu ne merites pas d'en manger.' (Chapter 3)

> 'I want some food'—'You don't deserve to eat.' (p.27)

He preaches whereas Jacques acts. His description of the Pope as the Antichrist emphasises the divisions in the Christian Church between Protestants and Catholics.

(2) The auto-da-fé shows the absurd superstition and cruelty of the Inquisition:

> ... il était decidé par l'université de Coïmbre que le spectacle de quelques personnes brûlées à petit feu, en grande cérémonie, est un secret infaillible pour empêcher la terre de trembler. (Chapter 6)

> The University of Coimbra had pronounced that the sight of a few people ceremoniously burned alive before a slow fire was an infallible prescription for preventing earthquakes. (p.36)

(3) Cunégonde's lovers are the Jewish banker to the court, Don Issachar, and the Catholic Inquisitor:

> Le juif aurait pour lui les lundis, mercredis et le jour du sabbat, et l'inquisiteur aurait les autres jours de la semaine. (Chapter 8)

I should belong to both of them in common, to the Jew on Mondays, Wednesdays and the Sabbath days, and to the Inquisitor the other days of the week. (p.42)

Thus members of both religions are equally immoral.

(4) A monk steals the jewels (Chapter 10). Similarly the Périgord priest deceives Candide and robs him (Chapter 22). Giroflée explains the misery of a monastery, where younger sons are sent to preserve the family inheritance for the eldest son:

La jalousie, la discorde, la rage, habitent dans le couvent. (Chapter 24)

As for the monastery, it is riddled with jealousy, discord and fury! (p.116)

(5) The old woman is 'the Pope's daughter', a comment on Catholic morality. She is crudely searched for diamonds by the Knights of St John, crusaders who abuse the vows of their religious order. The Moslems destroy her family and fight a civil war,

sans qu'on manquât aux cinq prières par jour ordonnées par Mahomet. (Chapter 11)

Yet they will not miss one of the five daily prayers prescribed by Mahomet (p.53)

—again, faith becomes a mere pantomime.

(6) Voltaire frequently satirises those who take the Bible literally. Pangloss's references to the Ancients (Chapter 30) and his genealogy of syphilis (Chapter 4) parody the Old Testament; similarly, Candide's inability to lie that Cunégonde is his sister, emphasises Abraham's dubious morality when he lied about Sarah. (Chapter 13)

(7) The religious war in Paraguay is an excuse for the Jesuits to take advantage of the natives, while pretending to practise Christianity:

Los Padres y ont tout, et les peuples rien; c'est le chef d'oeuvre de la raison et de la justice. (Chapter 14)

The reverend fathers own the whole lot, and the people own nothing: that's what I call a masterpiece of reason and justice. (p.62)

The Commandant says the Spanish will be 'excommunicated and beaten'. Voltaire detests the mixture of military and ecclesiastical styles, for the Church preaches love yet makes war. No wonder the Oreillons cry for joy:

Mangeons du jésuite! (Chapter 16)

We'll have Jesuit for dinner! (p.70)

(8) Eldorado contrasts utterly with the rest of the world. All is calm, prosperous and happy. There are no churches, no monks, no Inquisition, merely songs of praise to express thanks to God:

> Est-ce qu'il peut y avoir deux religions? Nous avons, je crois, la religion de tout le monde; nous adorons Dieu du soir jusqu'au matin. (Chapter 18)

> 'Can there be two religions, then?' said he. 'I have always believed that we hold the religion of all mankind. We worship God from morning till night.' (p.79)

(9) The Surinam slave sees how little notice the Dutch traders take of their religion:

> C'est à ce prix que vous mangez du sucre en Europe. (Chapter 19)

> That's the price of your eating sugar in Europe. (p.86)

(10) Religious intolerance deprives actresses of 'the honours of the tomb'; they are flung on the dung-heap. (Chapter 22)

(11) Strangers are arrested because of the fear of further assassination attempts on the King. (Chapter 22) These are the result of religious fanaticism.

(12) Paquette numbers a monk among her seducers (Chapter 24), and both a Franciscan and a Jesuit appear in Pangloss's genealogy of venereal disease. (Chapter 4) Throughout the novel men betray their religious vows.

THE SATIRE OF NATIONALISM

Voltaire also condemns excessive national pride. It is usually an excuse to murder the innocent and steal their land. Throughout the world Candide meets the same vanity in many different national guises. It is noticeable that in the most peaceful Kingdom, Eldorado, the King is the least vain of men and greets Candide as an equal.

(1) The Baron's 'castle' in Westphalia, with its door, windows and carpet, parodies all the petty German principalities. Voltaire ridicules their snobbery, when Candide's father is rejected for his 'mere' seventy-one quarterings.

(2) Such pride easily leads to war. The Bulgars' war against the Abars parodies Frederick the Great's war against France. The deceitful conscription of Candide, the appalling discipline and punishments, the

suffering of each village in turn, the 'heroes' who murder the innocent, the 'Te Deum' sung by both sides, all belie the seeming splendour of the battle:

> Les trompettes, les fifres, les hautbois, les tambours, les canons, formaient une harmonie telle qu'il n'y en eut jamais en enfer. (Chapter 3)

> Bugles, fifes, oboes, drums, and salvoes of artillery produced such a harmony as Hell itself could not rival. (p.25)

(3) The Paraguayan religious war emphasises the national greed of the colonial powers at the expense of the natives. Similarly the Moorish pirates and the Dutch slave trade suggest it is a universal evil. Indeed, Candide is cheated by people of so many different nationalities that clearly no country has much right to be at all proud of its inhabitants.

(4) When Admiral Byng is executed by the English, Voltaire condemns the absurdity of a colonial war:

> Vous savez que ces deux nations sont en guerre pour quelques arpents de neige vers le Canada, et qu'elles dépensent pour cette belle guerre beaucoup plus que tout le Canada ne vaut. (Chapter 23)

> You realise, of course, that these two nations are fighting over a few acres of snow on the borders of Canada, and that they spend more money on this glorious war than the whole of Canada is worth. (p.110)

(5) The fate of the Kings and the viziers in Constantinople emphasises that national pride and glory are precarious things. They remind Candide to concentrate on the essential virtues of life:

> 'Etes-vous roi aussi Monsieur?'—'Non, messieurs, et n'en ai nulle envie.' (Chapter 26)

> 'Are you also a King, sir?'—'No, sirs, nor do I wish to be.' (p.128)

THE SATIRE OF SOCIETY

(1) Eldorado is an idealised vision of a happy society. The King is democratic; the people choose to stay; there is no need for courts, parliaments or prisons; everyone is hospitable and grateful to God; scientific galleries lead to constant progress; and above all:

> Tous les hommes sont libres. (Chapter 18)

> All men are free! (p.83)

(2) This contrasts with Candide's experience of the real world. Paquette

symbolises human misery, for as a prostitute she is 'one of the unhappiest creatures alive' and can expect only:

   ... une vieilleuse affreuse, un hôpital, et un fumier. (Chapter 24)

   ... a terrible old age, the workhouse and the dunghill. (p.115)

The whole novel exposes the evils of society and, especially in Chapter 22, those of a big city.

(3) Nevertheless, Voltaire believes that society can be improved. He does not want to return to a primitive state, and mocks Rousseau's idea of the 'noble savage' in the scene with the girls and the monkeys. Instead, he wants to use what is best in man to build a happy, useful community as Candide does in Constantinople. Voltaire recognises a natural sense of justice in all men—Cacambo relies on this when he persuades the Oreillons to release him and Candide; and he has faith in man's powers of reason. Thus, if men will only be honest and charitable with each other, then they can make life generally pleasanter, even though natural disasters will always remain a threat. Then society will have a chance to prove itself. As Voltaire said in his poem on the Lisbon disaster,

   Un jour tout sera bien, voilà notre espérance.

   One day all will be well, that is our hope.

The satire in *Candide* certainly proves that it is an illusion that all is well now.

The structure

The 'conte', or short story, particularly suits Voltaire. He is not hampered by the rigid rules of classical tragedy or epic poetry; and in an imaginative, humorous disguise he can hide his rebellious thoughts.

If necessary, he can deny he wrote them at all and attribute them to 'Dr Ralph'! Above all, he can invent a cartoon world reminiscent of his magic lantern shows at Ferney. He bounces Candide from event to event and emotion to emotion like a ping-pong ball at such speed that we cannot take him too seriously. No one could really suffer so many disasters. Yet most people suffer some of his experiences, and even as we laugh, we remain aware that in real life such problems are not funny at all. The novel is so skilfully constructed, that we inevitably remain detached and therefore, even as we enjoy it, we preserve our objectivity.

Candide is at the centre of everything. Sometimes he experiences life at first hand, sometimes from the life-story of others; but everything is a stage along his path to maturity. Voltaire has carefully planned the route. First Candide moves westwards, only to find that the New World is as bad as the Old; he pauses at the mirage of Eldorado; and then he moves back eastwards, until at last he reaches his goal. The gardens provide a similarly balanced structure. At first he thinks Westphalia is the garden of Eden; then he finds a paradise on earth in Eldorado; and ends in a less exotic, but still fruitful garden by the Bosphorus. Even his innocent youth contrasts with the wise old age of the sages of Eldorado and Constantinople. Everything thus focuses our attention on Candide's intellectual development, and this ensures that we concentrate on the essential problem of optimism.

Candide's emotional development also lends shape to the novel. The terrified young man at the start becomes much more independent. Thus eventually he dismisses the Baron's son with a threat, and politely but firmly contradicts Pangloss. To begin with, Candide is excessively sensitive. He swoons at the sight of Cunégonde, is deliriously happy when he finds his llama in the sea, and is 'transported' at the very thought of seeing Cunégonde again. When he is not overjoyed, he is weeping profusely at each new disaster. Only when he settles down to work does he become much calmer. In his garden he achieves something of the serenity of Eldorado, whereas Pangloss's exaggerations encouraged the displays of emotion that left him ill prepared for real life. Again, Voltaire makes sure that we never lose sight of the essential theme of the book.

The other characters are puppets. This means we cannot become humanly involved in their problems. They remain comical caricatures, and we are again left free coolly to reflect on the real world. Most of them are mere types. Their very names emphasise the point. Candide is candid, Pangloss is all tongue, Pococurante cares little, Cunégonde is oversexed, Cacambo revels in the filth and beauty ('caca'-'beau') of life, Vanderdendur has 'hard teeth'. Men with a clear philosophy of life have simple names, like Jacques or Martin. Only the Spanish Don has several, and they match his pomposity. The rest are mere symbols without names at all, such as the Grand Inquisitor, the old woman, the Périgord priest, and so on. What is more, they are as indestructible as the heroes of any cartoon! It would be hard to say which is more implausible, the rainstorm that causes the clumsy hanging of Pangloss or the chance arrival of the King at Candide's execution. At least these are reasons of a sort, whereas the Baron's son, run through by Candide's sword, is simply 'cured'! We cannot take them seriously, and we judge as we laugh.

This is also true of the events that they undergo. Certainly they experience the earthquakes, pirates, cannibals, wars, shipwrecks, lost worlds, imprisonment and last minute rescues that belong to any adventure story. However, in most tales we share the thrills of our hero and suffer when he suffers. Here, though, there is simply too much, and anyway it is all too funny, to be possible. Even the historical events are sometimes deliberately unconvincing. There was no war at the time in Westphalia; and two of the Kings were dead at the time of the Venice carnival. An eighteenth century audience would appreciate these discrepancies more easily than we can now. Everything, then, alienates us from the action and enables us to weigh the value of Pangloss's teaching.

The style

The language itself illustrates Candide's progress towards maturity. As the compact, colourful, crisp sentences hurry him through life, the meaningless superlatives of his youth give way to a calm, reflective style.

Voltaire parodies the language of shallow philosophers. In their jargon everything is 'the best', 'the most beautiful', 'the most powerful' and so on. Frequently Voltaire uses a word diametrically the opposite of what he really means, such as 'harmony' or 'encourage', and if Pangloss proves a theory it is 'admirable'; in other words, he is destroying Pangloss with his own words. However, even Martin, though not nearly so silly, is also guilty of talking in unrealistically absolute terms. For example, he says that wherever one goes in France:

> . . . la principale occupation est l'amour; la seconde, de médire; et la troisième, de dire des sottises. (Chapter 21)

> the chief occupations are making love, backbiting, and talking nonsense. (p.94)

Pessimism emerges, then, as an equally dangerous philosophy, for it is also much too extreme and passive. Voltaire's own life refutes Martin's view of the French people; they are not *all* like that. Again, Pococurante's weary observations on the cultural world are equally absolute and many critics would question their validity.

All this contrasts with the simple, restrained style of the King of Eldorado:

> je sais bien que mon pays est peu de chose; mais, quand on est passablement quelque part, il faut y rester. (Chapter 18)

> I realise that my country is not much to boast of, but a man should be satisfied with what works moderately well. (p.83)

His modest description of perfection emphasises the superficiality of others' lordly claims.

Voltaire also parodies the excessively passionate language of the romantic novel. We have seen how Candide overreacts to any situation, until at last he acquires a sense of proportion. Voltaire often describes a situation in this breathless style; but then he invariably punctures the mood with a very prosaic observation. He will not let his characters linger in the airy, empty world of idealised passion, and brings them down to earth with an undignified bump. When Candide finds Cunégonde again, for example, Voltaire dwells on the same point until it becomes absurd:

> Quel moment! quelle surprise! il croit voir mademoiselle Cunégonde, il la voyait en effet, c'était elle-même! (Chapter 6)

> He had the surprise of his life, for to his astonished gaze it seemed that Lady Cunégonde stood before him. And so, in fact, she did. (p.39)

Similarly, he repeats the fact that they cannot speak, that they faint, chatter, sigh, weep and shout. The style is ecstatic, until Voltaire destroys the atmosphere with Cunégonde's fatuous remark that ravishing and disembowelling do not always kill you.

There are many such moments. When Candide loses Cunégonde to Don Fernando, for instance, he says he is utterly desperate. But:

> En parlant ainsi, il ne laissa pas de manger. (Chapter 16)

> While giving vent to these melancholy reflections, he was making a hearty meal. (p.69)

He clearly intends to prolong his 'miserable existence', whatever he may claim.

Indeed, Candide's first physical contact with Cunégonde amusingly illustrates Voltaire's technique. After their 'innocent' meeting:

> . . . leurs bouches se rencontrèrent, leurs yeux s'enflammèrent, leurs genoux tremblèrent . . . (Chapter 1)

> Their lips met, their eyes flashed, their knees trembled . . . (p.21)

—and we are swept into the traditionally passionate world of the trite romantic novel, until Voltaire concludes with the mildly vulgar sugsugestiveness of:

> . . . leurs mains s'égarèrent. (Chapter 1)
> . . . their hands would not keep still. (p.21)

Their wandering hands remind us that they are not really very bothered about the abstract theories of German philosophers.

Voltaire's style is animated by a sense of speed. The short sentences help to create the illusion of a cartoon chase. Phrases such as 'à peine' (hardly), 'déjà' (already) and 'après' (after) constantly hurry us on to the next incident.

The journey to Eldorado, though appallingly difficult, covers only a few lines. Dialogue constantly enlivens the narrative. Verb after verb keeps the story moving. There is no time to be bored; we are too busy wondering what will happen next.

Further variety is found in the moods that Voltaire evokes. Sheer farce and bleakest tragedy jostle together. From a thousand examples, let us compare two. Firstly, there is the absurdly illogical remark of the Baron's son:

Tu peux me tuer encore, mais tu n'épouseras pas ma soeur de mon vivant. (Chapter 29)

You can kill me again if you like, but while I live, you shall never marry my sister. (p.138)

Ludicrous it may be, but it is justified by the course of events, and delightfully captures the German's preposterous snobbery and obstinacy. How different is the tone of our second illustration. Candide is walking through the Abar village during the battle:

... d'autres, à demi brûlées, criaient qu'on achevât de leur donner la mort. Des cervelles étaient répandues sur la terre à côté de bras et de jambes coupés. (Chapter 3)

Others, whose bodies were badly scorched, begged to be put out of their misery. Whichever way he looked, the ground was strewn with the legs, arms and brains of dead villagers. (p.26)

There is nothing remotely funny about the harsh realism of this scene. Even more bitter is the anger we sense when Voltaire describes the outrageous treatment of the Surinam slave. Yet there is always someone as idiotic as Don Fernando to restore the humour. Voltaire's vivid style is a reflection of the variety of life itself.

Above all, Voltaire's ironic style exactly suits the practical attitude to life that he consistently advocates. It underlines his warnings to us to be on our guard against charlatans. So many things in 'Candide' prove to be false on closer examination. For instance, so many people behave politely to Candide at first, only to emerge as his enemies. The soldiers are charmingly hospitable to him, until they have press-ganged him; so is the officer of the Inquisition who arrests him; so too the Périgord priest who robs him. No wonder that Candide exclaims:

Si c'est ici le meilleur des mondes possibles, que sont donc les autres? (Chapter 6)

If this is the best of all possible worlds, what can the rest be like? (p.37)

Humbug is defenceless against Voltaire's irony. Yet he uses it only to clear the ground for positive action. When at the very last Candide says:

... il faut cultiver notre jardin (Chapter 30)

... we must go and work in the garden. (p.144)

there is not a trace of irony. It is no longer necessary, for Candide has learnt his lesson.

Part 4

Hints for study

Points for detailed study

The first thing to think about is the humour. After all, the novel condemns those who live in a theoretical world. It would be sad to reduce *Candide* to an abstract thesis and to miss all the colour and entertainment.

Look, then, at the variety of comic techniques. The characterisation, the structure and the style each display astonishing versatility. The characters, for instance, represent different points of view, and we should see how their funny names and their predictable behaviour create the atmosphere of a cartoon. We should particularly notice how often they give themselves away in conversation: Cunégonde, for example, cannot conceal her sensuality; the Baron's son tries to hide his homosexuality in bombastic protests; and above all, Pangloss clearly knows he is wrong, but cannot admit it.

The comedy of situation also creates a zany world. Much of it is farcical. The 'experimental physics', the eunuch's frustration, the Pope's daughter's missing buttock, or the monkeys and the naked girls are cheerful, vulgar fun.

Equally attractive are the unashamedly unconvincing coincidences that occur all through the book. So too are the preposterously narrow escapes, such as that of Pangloss after he is taken to the mortuary. At other times, though, the comedy of situation has a bitter taste. There is a certain grim humour, when both kings sing a victory hymn or when a second earthquake follows the auto-da-fé, but we can only afford a wry smile in the face of man's cruelty to man.

The language emulates this broad range of mood. Some is simple mockery. The German names, for instance, parody the guttural sounds of the language. Such gentle irony typifies the satire of the breathless ecstasy of the lovers or the empty superlatives of the optimists. At other moments, though, we sense the fierce indignation behind the irony. The 'price of sugar in Europe' is human blood, and the sardonic wit makes no attempt to conceal the horror.

Never forget that *Candide* is funny, then, not just because if you do, you run the risk of being another Pangloss yourself, but because the humour has a very practical role to play. It enables us to stand back from the action and judge not so much the characters, for they are a joke, as the ideas they represent, for these are real and can do much good or evil.

Now you should reflect on these ideas. We saw in Part 3 that Voltaire satirises extremism. Try to find more examples of his parody of philosophy, religion, politics and society.

By now, you will have a clear idea of what Voltaire is saying. Ask yourself the most important question of all. Is it worth saying? It clearly was so, in the eighteenth century. It epitomised Voltaire's aspirations for France and for mankind. Has the book become another unread, dusty volume on the shelves of some twentieth-century Pococurante? If it made you laugh, then that alone justifies its existence. On a deeper level, though, we should ask whether *Candide* has any application to modern life.

Voltaire satirises the passive philosophies of optimism and pessimism. Not many would now claim that this world is ideal; but under the threat of nuclear war we must carefully consider Martin's view of life. Is it still worth while digging our garden? It remains 'a big question'. Voltaire also satirises those who fail to practise the loving charity that they preach in their religions. Is the world yet purged of such hypocrites? He satirises the nationalist ambitions of tyrants. Are the political leaders of today any less greedy than they were, and are politicians any more straightforward? Eldorado still seems remote. Lastly, Voltaire satirises society. Are we yet cured of the evils of prostitution? Venereal disease may have been controlled, but are drugs and alcohol any less a threat to sanity and health? Pirates now carry bombs and hijack planes. Giroflée might not now enter a monastery, but how many clerks and labourers are forced to do jobs they hate? Above all, how many people are brave enough to tell the truth all the time? That day when 'all will be well' is still a long way off, and *Candide* poses problems instantly recognisable to all men at all times.

The selection of suitable quotations

Almost every line of *Candide* is memorable, but clearly some choice is necessary in an essay. If you have to discuss the ideas, you can often let a character speak for himself, for he will typify one point of view. If you have to analyse the style, concentrate on the contrasts, for these animate the story and create an atmosphere of debate. Thus pomposity is matched by sincerity, tragedy by comedy, cruelty by tenderness, confusion by calm, and fantasy by reason.

Every detail contributes something positive to the story. You can show this best by analysing a substantial section of the text. The start of Chapter 3, for example, is in many ways a miniature of the whole novel:

Rien n'était si beau, si leste, si brillant, si bien ordonné que les deux armées. Les trompettes, les fifres, les hautbois, les tambours, les canons, formaient une harmonie telle qu'il n'y en eut jamais en enfer. Les canons renversèrent d'abord à peu près six mille hommes de chaque côté; ensuite la mousqueterie ôta du meilleur des mondes environ neuf à dix mille coquins qui en infectaient la surface. La baïonnette fut aussi la raison suffisante de la mort de quelques milliers d'hommes. Le tout pouvait bien se monter à une trentaine de mille âmes. Candide, qui tremblait comme un philosophe, se cacha du mieux qu'il put pendant cette boucherie héroïque.

Those who have never seen two well-trained armies drawn up for battle, can have no idea of the beauty and brilliance of the display. Bugles, fifes, oboes, drums, and salvoes of artillery produced such a harmony as Hell itself could not rival. The opening barrage destroyed about six thousand men on each side. Rifle-fire which followed rid this best of worlds of about nine or ten thousand villains who infested its surface. Finally, the bayonet provided 'sufficient reason' for the death of several thousand more. The total casualties amounted to about thirty thousand. Candide trembled like a philosopher, and hid himself as best he could during this heroic butchery.

When you write a critical appreciation, you should first state the context, for the position of the passage is often very significant. After all, this description of the Abar-Bulgar War would lose much of its impact if it occurred later in the novel. Candide's trust in Pangloss is still total when he is abruptly confronted with warfare, the ultimate horror that men can inflict upon each other. Thus Voltaire at once sets the theory of optimism in dramatic conflict with the harsh realities of life, and the implications are devastating.

Next, you want to decide upon the main theme of the passage under examination. If it is well written, every detail will in some way relate to this central idea: if not, some phrases will be exposed as mere padding. This theme should in turn be linked to the main idea of the work; such concentric circles display the artistic unity of the novel. The most obvious example of this is seen in any extract from the section on Eldorado, where the essential idea is that reasonable behaviour creates social harmony. This in turn has a clear bearing on the rest of the book, for by contrast it emphasises the untruthfulness of Pangloss's claim that all is for the best. In our passage from Chapter 3, the essential idea is the satire of war: Voltaire contrasts the glorious appearance with the monstrous reality. This, then, exactly mirrors the principal message of the novel, for time and again people, institutions, places and things prove to be worse than they seem, just as Pangloss glosses over the true facts.

This introduction to your commentary should be very succinct. Do not waste time retelling the plot, for the reader, probably an examiner, knows that well enough. State the context briefly, elucidate the themes concisely, and concentrate on explaining the significance of each statement you make. It is pointless, for instance, just to observe that Voltaire describes the beauty of an army drawn up for battle. Anyone can see that for himself. Your task is to say *why* Voltaire describes this beauty. The answer, of course, is that he is being sarcastic, and that such beauty reflects the pompous vanity of kings, whose ambition causes untold misery to ordinary, innocent people. In other words, this passage is not about beauty at all, but about something profoundly ugly.

It is helpful if you also mention the tone of the passage. If Jacques is speaking, we can take his words at their face value, for he is sincere even unto death. However, when the Baron's son justifies his 'innocent' swim with the page-boy, we know his sexual inclinations well enough by now to view his righteous indignation with suspicion! In other words, you must say if Voltaire is being ironic or not. In our passage from Chapter 3 he varies the mood radically. He begins with a sunny optimism that parodies Pangloss's style; deflates it with his own sarcasm; and concludes with a brutal realism that shows where his sympathies really lie. His irony is everywhere apparent.

Now you must explain the point of any detail that is worthy of comment. Do it systematically. You might, for example, work your way steadily through the text, following the excellent French method of 'explication'; or if you prefer, pick out examples that relate to a particular theme. For instance, phrases such as 'sufficient reason', 'best of worlds' and 'cause and effect' belong to the jargon of Leibniz and Wolff, and you can briefly explain them and relate them to the satire of pedantic optimists. Again, explain what is meant by a 'Te Deum': it is a hymn that thanks God for victory; you can therefore show how Voltaire is satirising both war and religion. Both kings cannot have won the battle, and certainly there is no sense of religion in such wholesale slaughter. This in turn reminds us that Voltaire does not believe that God is concerned with the wars of petty humanity. Keep such comments crisp. If you do not, you will end up with an unbalanced essay, and lose sight of another very necessary task.

This is to evaluate the style. The passage opens with cheerful confidence. 'Rien' (nothing) is so brilliant as the sight of the army: a statement of absolute certainty, typical of the superlatives of Pangloss. The repetition of 'so' before each adjective has a pleasingly harmonious sound that matches the military music. Then suddenly Voltaire's sarcasm breaks through. This is a harmony unknown even in Hell—of course it is only harmonious if we believe that it fits into a world where all is already ideal; and no one can seriously maintain that a battle is in fact harmonious. In other words, the original absolute confidence is nonsensical. As so often, Voltaire uses a word that says precisely the opposite of what he really means. To 'encourage the others' meant to 'discourage' them. Now 'harmony' means 'chaos'. The style is not only grimly humorous, it also encourages us to delve into the real significance of words.

The tenses of the verbs are always significant. The imperfect tense is used to set the scene. The sudden past historic of 'renversèrent' (destroyed) abruptly recalls us from airy fantasy to the hard facts of war. The battlefield is evoked with remarkable economy. In a mere four lines .Voltaire mentions the canons, the rifles and the bayonets: in other words, from the first salvo to the hand-to-hand fighting, normally a matter of hours, only seconds seem to have elapsed. Like a figure in a cartoon, Candide is whirled round in helpless confusion.

Words such as 'infect' deliberately reduce man to a mere germ in this 'best of worlds'; but by now the irony is apparent, and when we reflect on the appalling loss of human life, we realise that it is the rulers that infect their people, and not the people who infect a world that is anything but 'the best'. The numbers, too, have a cold bureaucratic ring about them, reducing men to mere targets to be fired at. The cynical phrase 'heroic butchery', reduces an epic battle to the level of a slaughterhouse, coldly exposing the tyranny of the kings who caused such cruelty.

When Candide trembles 'like a philosopher', Voltaire amusingly ridicules those who talk grandly but cannot cope with real life; the moment anticipates Pangloss's useless behaviour amidst the ruins of Lisbon. After another satirical allusion to Pangloss's jargon, Candide sees the true horrors of war. Piles of bodies and smoking ruins lie all around him. This leads on to a picture of agony, but our passage ends with the bitterly ironic observation that it is all in accordance with the 'droit public' ('the terms of international law'). Again the phrase suggests harmony and justice for all men, and yet means exactly the reverse.

In your concluding paragraph it would be useful to show how this passage is an integral part of the whole chapter. Candide will find exactly the same suffering in the enemy village. All men, then, have a capacity for savagery, if they fail to use their reason. Moreover, you should point out that this passage, an example of universal misery, leads on to one of personal sorrow, when the Dutch preacher abuses Candide. Yet neither experience is sufficient to dampen his faith in Pangloss, for Jacques' kindness immediately restores it. The chapter comes full circle with the return of Pangloss. The opening section of Chapter 3 destroys Pangloss's theory of optimism. The grotesque, decaying apparition at the end of this chapter vividly illustrates the downfall not just of the man but of his philosophy of life.

Specimen questions

Whichever essay you are required to write, you must have a plan. Begin by analysing the title. For example, you might be asked to discuss Voltaire's own description of himself: 'One of those little brooks that are very clear, because they are not very deep'. Two essential features emerge from this: firstly, Voltaire claims that his ideas are superficial, and secondly, that because of this they are easy to comprehend. Now *Candide* discusses deism, optimism and pessimism; it considers social iniquity on a world-wide scale; and it offers a creative philosophy of life. These are 'very deep' matters, and Voltaire is being disarmingly modest. However, the rich variety of his style, and the biting accuracy of his ironic observations, ensure that his ideas are quickly understood. We should not confuse solemnity with profundity. Pangloss is very pedantic, but his thoughts are shallow; Voltaire is very funny, but that does not prevent him from thinking clearly.

Once you have thoroughly grasped the point of the question that you have to answer, then, and only then, you can follow the plan of your essay. The topic in our illustration now falls neatly into two parts: firstly, the meaning of the novel; and secondly, its artistic merit. You should subdivide these two sections into more manageable paragraphs. To find the meaning, you need to examine: firstly, the philosophical ideas; secondly, the religious ones; thirdly, the political ones; and fourthly, the social ones. In other words, all those things that Voltaire is satirising. To analyse the artistry, you should examine: the style of the language; the structure of the story; and the characterisation. In other words, you will show the skill and humour with which Voltaire makes the points you noted in the first part of the essay. Each of these sections may be subdivided for the sake of clarity. An obvious case, for example, is the characterisation, where you might look at those characters, such as Candide, whose personalities develop; then at those who are mere caricatures. Alternatively, you might consider those who are the objects of ridicule, such as Pangloss and the Baron's son, and then those whom we should respect, such as the King of Eldorado and the old man in Constantinople.

There is no one answer to a literary essay. What matters is to be clear, and, as Pococurante rightly suggests, to say what you honestly think. It would be absurd not to give your sincere opinions on *Candide*, when the whole book is an appeal for sincerity and freedom of expression. A final paragraph can round off the essay, summing up the principal points, and perhaps opening the reader's mind to wider horizons. For instance, you might pursue the image of the brook, and suggest that Voltaire's novel is no mere stream, but a broad, deep river that has flowed across the world and across the centuries, for the humour has retained its freshness, the problems are as vital as ever to mankind, and in the confusion and anxiety of the modern world, we more than ever require the clarity of vision and of diction that are to be found in the work of Voltaire.

Other essays may be more straightforward. For instance, you might be asked to analyse the character of Pococurante. Obviously you must illustrate carefully the different opinions he reveals in the text. However, the essay becomes much more convincing if you relate all your examples to the essential nature of his character. His name emphasises his fundamental disillusionment with life. This in turn becomes far more significant, if, at the start of your essay, you explain how such an attitude is proof that all is not well with the world. Candide learns that hard work is the antidote to misery, vice and boredom. Pococurante, then, is much more than an entertaining episode in Candide's life; he is an integral part of his education.

Other essay titles may take a provocative stance. For example, 'Candide is a work of total pessimism. Discuss.' First of all, be careful at all times to distinguish between Candide, the novel, and Candide, the character, for if you do not make it plain when you are writing about the novel and not the character you may well seem to be saying something you do not mean. To take a very simple example, if you say that Candide is naïve, this is true, but in no way is Candide naïve, it is the result of deep reflection upon bitter experience.

Again, we must look carefully at the title. Much in the novel is pessimistic and explains Martin's gloom. The essay should, then, examine all those features of the ideas, the characterisation, the structure and the style that are pessimistic, and then those that are not. Since the final chapter offers a measure of hope, we may conclude that the novel is not totally pessimistic. That can be shown. A much more taxing essay, though, will ask whether Candide is more pessimistic than optimistic. The essay will follow a similar pattern to the previous one, but this time the conclusion will depend on the reader's personal opinion. Never be afraid to disagree with the statement in the title. Sift all the evidence and decide for yourself.

Other essay titles to consider with reference to Candide include:
(a) 'Candide is paradoxically a work of optimism.' Discuss.
(b) 'Voltaire's philosophy is largely a matter of ethics and social reform.' Discuss.
(c) Analyse Voltaire's attitude to religion.
(d) 'The tale is really only a vehicle for the author's propaganda.' Discuss.

(e) 'In this book the horror of evil and an instinctive zest for life are almost equally matched.' Discuss.

(f) 'The story is constructed with deceptive skill.' Discuss.

(g) 'The novel has inevitably dated.' Discuss.

(h) Analyse Voltaire's attitude to extremists.

(i) Analyse the prose style.

(j) Examine Voltaire's irony.

(k) Discuss the humour in the novel.

(l) How does the novel anticipate the cartoon film?

(m) Discuss Voltaire's use of history.

(n) How does he parody the romantic novel?

(o) How does he parody the picaresque novel?

(p) Discuss the symbolic value of the characters.

(q) 'It is often alleged that for all their beauties, Voltaire's stories are deficient in characterisation.' (Besterman). Discuss.

(r) Discuss Voltaire's use of local colour to evoke an atmosphere.

(s) Consider his attitude to national characteristics.

(t) What is the significance of the Lisbon earthquake?

(u) What is the significance of Eldorado?

(v) What is the significance of the final chapter?

(w) How does the novel reflect the author's own experiences?

(x) Tolstoy says of the German commander Pfuel in 1806 in *War and Peace*, Book 9, Chapter 11:

> His love of theory made him hate everything practical and he would not listen to it. He was even pleased by failure, for failures resulting from deviations in practice from the theory, only proved to him the accuracy of his theory.

How relevant is this to the parody of Wolff?

(y) Which philosophers does Voltaire satirise and with what success?

(z) 'Voltaire is the initiator of the modern world.' (Benda). Discuss.

Part 5

Suggestions for further reading

The text

There are many good critical editions of *Candide*, including:

(*a*) in French: *Candide, édition critique*, edited by René Pomeau, Nizet, Paris, 1959. *Candide, édition abrégée*, edited by André Séailles, Nouveaux Classiques Larousse, Paris, 1970.

(*b*) in English: *Voltaire's Candide*, edited by J. H. Brumfitt, Oxford University Press, London, 1968.

Other works by Voltaire

(*a*) For an idea of Voltaire's extraordinary diversity, the following might be selected from his *Complete Works*:

Lettres philosophiques (first published in England in 1733 as *Letters Concerning the English Nation*).

Tancrède (1760), the tragedy that moves Candide to tears.

La Henriade (1728), Voltaire's epic poem.

Le siècle de Louis XIV (1751), the work of the royal historian.

Dr Besterman has launched the definitive edition of Voltaire's complete works. All the above texts are easily found in individual editions as well.

(*b*) *Candide* will almost certainly whet the appetite for other tales. Again there are many editions. Two well presented volumes are:

(*i*) in French: *Voltaire: Romans et Contes*, introduced by Roland Barthes, Gallimard, Paris, 1972.

(*ii*) in English: *Zadig and other stories*, edited by H. T. Mason, Clarendon French Series, Oxford University Press, London, 1971.

These are not only delightful to read, but afford a very stimulating comparison with the themes and style of *Candide*.

Biography

BESTERMAN, THEODORE: *Voltaire*, Longmans, London, 1969. This is the best book to read on Voltaire's life and times. Dr Besterman lived in Voltaire's home at Les Délices, was Director of the Institut et Musée Voltaire and writes with a grace, clarity and wit that matches Voltaire's own.

Criticism

BARBER, W.H.: *Voltaire: Candide* (Studies in French Literature) Edward Arnold, London, 1960.

The two texts that shed most light on the background to the philosophy of *Candide* are:

Essay on Man (1733–4) by Alexander Pope, in which he states the philosophy of optimism, and:

Poème sur le désastre de Lisbonne (1756) by Voltaire, in which he refutes the theory.

Both are readily available in many editions of their works.

The author of these notes

COLIN NIVEN was educated at Dulwich College, and Gonville and Caius College, Cambridge, where he read Modern and Medieval languages. He has a Diploma in Education from the University of Oxford, where he was at Brasenose College. He has taught frequently in Germany and France, including a spell at the Lycée mixte, Châlons-sur-Marne. In Great Britain he has taught at Samuel Pepys Comprehensive, Sedbergh and Fettes, where he was a Housemaster. During the Bicentennial he was the English Speaking Union Bell Tower scholar in the USA. He is currently Head of Modern Languages at Sherborne School.